SWING TRADING MADE SIMPLE:

Beginners Guide to the Best Strategies, Tools and Tactics to Profit from Outstanding Short-Term Trading Opportunities on Stock Market, Options, Forex, and Crypto

By

Richard Godwin

Table of Contents

Introduction.. 6

Chapter 1: An Overview of the Investment World .. 10

Where Did Modern Finance Come From?........................ 10

The Many Different Ways You Can Invest Your Money.... 13

Investments that May Be of Interest to Swing Traders..... 17

Exchange-Traded Funds.. 19

Commodities and Futures Markets 20

Trading in Stocks and Bonds 22

Options Trading 23

FOREX Trading 24

Chapter 2: What is Swing Trading? 25

What is Day Trading? 25

Swing Trading vs. Day Trading..................................... 27

What Instruments Can You Trade In With Swing
Trading? 30

Chapter 3: Market Signals.................................... 31

Candlesticks 33

Indecision Candles... 41

Oscillators 42

Support and Resistance 47

What Drives Market Momentum................................... 51

Looking for Uptrends.. 51

Downtrends.. 56

Flags 57

Moving Averages... 59

The Rule for Moving Averages 62

Types of Moving Averages 63

Exponential Moving Average 65

The Golden Cross 68

Death Cross 69

Chapter 4: 10 Top Swing Trading Strategies 73

Trendline Trading Strategy 73

Floor Trader Method 75

Supertrend 78

Gartley 79

Bollinger Bands and Dynamic Support and Resistance 81

Middle Bollinger Band FOREX Trading Strategy 87

CCI Moving Average Forex Trading Strategy 89

Picking Tops and Bottoms Trading Strategy Using ADX Indicator 90

The Hull Moving Average 91

Chapter 5: Safe Practices to Protect Your Capital .. 94

Only risk 1% of your capital on a trade 95

Stop-Loss Orders 97

Have preset profits in mind 98

Diversify your investments 100

Chapter 6: Swing Trading Cryptocurrency 101

Finding an exchange 101

Actually managing cryptocurrency 102

Trading on an Exchange 103

Trading using Robinhood 104

Chapter 7: Options Trading................................ 105

What is an Option? 105

Put Options 108

Maximum Losses 109

Tools to Use Trading Options 109

When are Options Out of the Money? 110

Time Horizons for Options 111

A Good Way to Learn Swing Trading 111

Buying Puts and Calls 112

Chapter 8: FOREX Trading Basics 114

How Currency is Traded 114

Profits in Pips.. 116

Currency Pairs and Charts 117

Swing Trading Forex.. 117

Chapter 9: Top Beginner Mistakes 118

Having unrealistic expectations................................. 118

Not treating trading like a business.............................118

Being too anxious... 119

Failing to Plan 120

Looking for a get rich quick scheme 120

Being put off by all that math 120

Losing control with leverage...................................... 121

Not relying on multiple indicators..............................122

**Chapter 10: How Much Money Do You Need to Get
Started 123**

Minimal Capital Requirements....................................123

Consider Options Trading..126

Planning for Risk 127

Bottom Line – How Much Do You Need? 130

Using Leverage 131

One Danger with Stop-Loss Orders 133

Chapter 11: Exchange-Traded Funds 134

Where to Buy Exchange-Traded Funds 135

Trading Options on Exchange-Traded Funds 136

iShares and SPDR 136

Summary 138

Conclusion 140

6

recorded copy and is only allowed with the express written consent from the Publisher. All additional right reserved.

The information in the following pages is broadly considered a truthful and accurate account of facts and as such, any inattention, use, or misuse of the information in question by the reader will render any resulting actions solely under their purview. There are no scenarios in which the publisher or the original author of this work can be in any fashion deemed liable for any hardship or damages that may befall them after undertaking information described herein.

Additionally, the information in the following pages is intended only for informational purposes and should thus be thought of as universal. As befitting its nature, it is presented without assurance regarding its prolonged validity or interim quality. Trademarks that are mentioned are done without written consent and can in no way be considered an endorsement from the trademark holder.

Introduction

Welcome to Swing Trading 2019: Beginners Guide to Best Strategies, Tools, Tactics and Psychology to Profit from Outstanding Short-Term Trading Opportunities on Stock Market, Options, Forex, and Cryptocurrencies!

In this book, we are going to introduce you to the exciting world of swing trading.

Swing trading is an interesting middle ground between day traders who take the most active role in trading along with the highest risk, and traditional investing which for many people simply means buy and hold until you're retired. Unlike day trading, swing trading doesn't have large capital requirements to get started, and it generally has lower levels of risk than day trading. You can get more involved in the market and look to make short-term profits, without being in the heart pumping world of day trading, where you can lose your shirt...in a day!

In this book, we are going to explain the basics of swing trading for the newbie. After a quick overview of investing in general, we'll start by explaining what swing trading is, and how it really differs from day trading. You'll then learn what instruments are best suited for swing trading, and how to develop a plan and mitigate your risks.

Then we'll cover the top strategies used by successful swing traders. You'll learn multiple methods, techniques to control your risk, and the basics of fundamental analysis that will help you estimate which direction security is heading.

Remember that any investing carries inherent financial risk. Never risk more capital than you can afford to lose. The techniques described in this book, while used by successful traders, cannot guarantee profits.

Chapter 1: An Overview of the Investment World

In this chapter, we're going to examine the world of investing briefly. We'll quickly discuss what types of investments are available, and the different methods used to manage investments, which include everything from simply putting your money into a mutual fund, all the way to being an active day trader moving tens of thousands of dollars per day. Once we establish the general context, then you'll have a solid understanding of where swing trading fits in.

Where Did Modern Finance Come From?

The history of financial markets begins with the concept of debt. Borrowing has been regulated since ancient times. Indeed, the first recorded instance of interest rates dates to 1800 BC, when a civilization in the Middle East known as the Hammurabi began regulating loans. At the time, people often borrowed money in order to purchase grain. People were already charging interest rates, but at this time, the authorities stepped in and imposed a limit on the interest rate that could be charged. They set the rate at 33 1/3 percent. This simple development illustrates that by 1800 BC, mathematical finance was already coming into existence. Various budding civilizations already had the

10

concept of principal, the amount of money borrowed, and interest to be added on when the principal was paid back. This basic form of debt and repayment of loans continues to survive to the modern day.

Fast forward to the Roman Empire, and the notion of selling and trading shares was born. The Romans often used private contractors to perform government services, including tax collection. The operators of these services used a modern technique of raising capital – they sold shares in the operation to the public. No doubt in those days, only elites could afford to buy such shares, but as soon as they become available, people began to trade the shares themselves. This raises an interesting point. Stock and trading markets are often viewed as a form of "capitalism," but ancient Rome certainly wasn't a capitalist society in the modern sense of the word. It seems that trading things – even financial instruments – is simply a trait all humans possess. Although the Romans began this practice after the empire disintegrated, it didn't continue, and so it's not seen as the root of modern finance.

To understand where modern finance came from, we fast forward to the Middle Ages. During that time, trading fairs became popular in Europe as a way for merchants to gather and sell or trade their goods. Governments also looked favorably on these trading fairs, allowing merchants to escape the normal taxes and duties applied to the sale of goods. It was here that currency trading and loans began, with many merchants at the fairs simply trading money or lending money.

At about the same time, lenders developed the concept of a mortgage, allowing people to borrow money in order to buy a property. Annuity contracts were also a large part of finance in the Middle Ages — that is, a person could buy an annuity and then receive lifetime payments in exchange. Obviously, this would have only been available to a small percentage of people alive at the time who would be able to purchase the annuity in the first place.

Bond trading began in Italy during the 1500s. Governments began to sell bonds, which would guarantee the holder of the bond payments in the form of interest over the lifetime of the bond. In the same way that people began trading shares in Roman tax collecting entities, people began buying and selling bonds.

During the age of exploration, when European countries were busily launching sea voyages, the modern concept of shares of stock was born. While it had some similarities to the shares created during Roman times, as far as we know, the idea was created independently in the 17th and 18th centuries. Holland played a major role in early sea voyages but putting together a sea voyage to distant lands was an extremely expensive endeavor, beyond even the richest individuals in Europe at the time. So in order to raise money for these voyages, the Dutch East India company was formed which sold shares of stock in the company. This was soon followed by the development of the first stock markets. It's not a coincidence that the modern stock exchange was founded in New York. When the Dutch owned what is now New York City, the Dutch governor order a wall to be built to protect the settlers from the British and Native Americans in the area. Soon afterward, the location became a favorite spot for traders, and of course, that has continued right through today.

The Many Different Ways You Can Invest Your Money

The modern world of finance and investing has been in place in the same basic form that we know it today for more than 100 years, although there are definitely new innovations that open up new opportunities, like the creation of derivative contracts and cryptocurrencies. Let's quickly review the ways that you can park your money and hopefully earn something off the money. We will go from more conservative (low risk) options to ways to invest that carry more risk but offer far more reward.

Ever since money was invented, people looked for ways to "save" money. It would be helpful to have money around in the future in case you ran into an emergency, such as needing to buy food. Or perhaps you didn't earn enough money to make a large purchase like a house, but you could save a little bit each month and build up the funds over time. While many fools have often stuffed money in their mattress, the most basic way to save money is to open a savings account in a bank. A savings account is one way that a bank can raise capital so that it can lend cash to others, so banks pay interest on the money in your savings account. Interest can be seen as the *cost of money*, so the cost to the bank is the interest that they pay you for parking your cash in their bank. When you borrow money from the bank, the interest you pay the bank is your cost of money. Banks also have different ways to invest in order to earn higher interest rates, such as money market funds and CDs. Unfortunately, due to many developments over the past several years, interest rates are quite low and putting your money in the bank isn't a good strategy for increasing your capital.

From here we move to bonds. The safest bonds that you can invest in are those issued by the United States government. The federal government issues four basic types of securities, treasury bonds, treasury bills, treasury notes, and TIPS, which are inflation protected treasuries. A bond has a face or par value and pays interest in exchange for the money used to purchase the bond. An interest payment on a bond is termed a "coupon payment." The lifetime of a bond is called maturity. That's a date in the future when the holder of the bond turns it in for payment. Of course, like anything else, bonds are traded on secondary markets.

- Treasury Bills: This is a short-term investment. These bonds expire in terms of 52 weeks, 26 weeks, 13 weeks, 8 weeks, and 4 weeks. You don't receive regular interest payments with treasury bills. Instead, they are sold at a discount, and then when the term of the bond is over, you are paid the full par value of the bond. To illustrate (with ridiculous interest rates), imagine that a bond had a par value of $100. The government would sell it to you for $75; then when you collected on the bond, they would pay you $100.

- Treasury Notes: A treasury note is a midterm bond in between Treasury Bills and long-term investments. You can purchase Treasury notes in terms of 2, 3, 5, 7, and 10 years. When you purchase a Treasury Note, you will receive a coupon payment every six months.

- Treasury Bonds: A treasury bond has a long lifetime of 30 years.

The interest paid on bonds is often expressed as the yield. The prices of bonds on secondary markets vary inversely with the current yield or interest rate. Imagine that a bond is issued that has an interest rate of 5%. Later, the interest rate drops to 3%. The bond is now worth more money since it pays a higher rate of interest than what a buyer could get buying a brand-new bond. Therefore, a trader can play the market by purchasing a bond at what they believe to be paying a higher interest rate than what will be paid in the future, and then they can sell the bond for a profit.

Conversely, if you buy a bond that pays 3% interest, and later the interest rate rises to 5%, the price of the bond will drop. The reason is that investors can buy new bonds and get a higher interest rate, so they have little incentive in buying an older bond that pays a lower rate.

You can buy and sell bonds directly, or you can invest in funds that manage bonds. The value of the fund will fluctuate based on its holding and the underlying situation for each bond that we described above. You can invest in mutual funds for this purpose or in exchange-traded funds (see below). Investors who are conservative tend to use investments in bond funds to protect part of their portfolio (i.e., protect the capital against loss; you always get the principal back with a bond). As people age, they tend to move more money into conservative investments like money market funds and bonds.

Next, we come to investments in mutual funds. Mutual funds are securities built up by pooling the money of many investors into a single fund, which can then invest in different securities such as stocks and bonds. In fact, mutual funds can invest in just about anything, including gold, commodities, stocks, stock market indexes, and bonds. However, these are investment vehicles used mainly by conservative minded individuals who are planning for their retirement. This is not going to be something a swing trader is going to be looking at. Mutual funds are usually managed by a supposedly "professional manager" who charges expensive fees for the privilege, although these days unmanaged funds with smaller fees are available. Mutual funds don't trade like stocks. Their price per share is settled after the close of each trading day. So a mutual fund by definition cannot take advantage of any price swings that occur during trading.

Beyond this, there are retirement vehicles like 401k's and IRA's that people who want to save up money for retirement can utilize. These can be composed of stock market investments, bonds, cash, and other types of investments. Typically, most people don't pay much attention to what goes on with their retirement accounts, so they are not a topic of interest for swing trading.

Investments that May Be of Interest to Swing Traders

At this point, we've finished the ways someone with a conservative mindset would invest their money. People with that mindset are looking for a retirement savings account, regardless of how that account is constructed in detail. A day or swing trader, by contrast, is looking to profit from short-term trends in the market. While someone putting money in mutual funds can be seen as an investor, a day or swing trader is more of a "speculator" that is running a business for profit. Keep in mind that speculator does not mean gambler. When you speculate on the market, you make educated guesses based on real-world data and rules about what that data means; you are not simply going with a hunch in your gut and hoping for fast profits.

But before we get to day and swing trading in detail, let's have a look at someone who actively invests in stocks, but is a "long-term" type of investor. This person may invest in multiple areas, such as stocks and bonds and maybe even metals, but they will do it with an eye on a long-time horizon, or at a minimum of three to five years. Normally it's a horizon of ten years or longer. So, it's a kind of variation on the idea of building up retirement savings, except that these people actively trade stocks and other investments. For the most part, they will purchase investments with an eye on the long-term outcome.

One technique that is used is "dollar cost averaging." While the day or swing trader attempts to profit from the wild swings that the chaotic stock market makes on a routine basis, an investor who uses dollar cost averaging aims to smooth out those swings. As an example, suppose that you were an investor who was bullish on Amazon. In that case, you would buy a given number of shares on a monthly basis no matter what was happening to the price. Some months the price would be up, some months the price will be down. The idea is to average out the ups and downs and profit on the holdings in Amazon that you'll have over a twenty- or thirty-year time period. When you're in retirement, then you'll slowly sell the stock to get cash to live on.

An investor using this type of strategy will use it even when the market is crashing in a recession. Buying securities during an economic downturn is, of course, an investment opportunity since they are going to be worth quite a bit more in the future. This will hold true in most cases, especially when we are talking about a long-time horizon of ten years or more.

Exchange-Traded Funds

Exchange-traded funds deserve a special mention because as a swing trader, you'll be interested in trading exchange-traded funds nearly as much as a conservative investor. An exchange-traded fund basically took the concept of a mutual fund and turned it into a stock. So, it's a pooled amount of money used to invest in actual securities. One example is SPY and exchange-traded fund that invests in the companies that make up the S & P 500. Since SPY is made up of the S & P 500, it tracks it quite closely. The pool of money used to make up the SPY fund is divided up into shares, which are then traded on the stock market in the same way that shares of Tesla or Apple are traded. Unlike a mutual fund, which is dormant during the day and has a price settlement once each business day after market close, exchange-traded funds are actively traded on the stock markets. This makes them of special interest for both day traders and swing traders. By using exchange-traded funds, you can profit on everything from the Dow Jones Industrial Average to gold or even real estate. You can also invest in newer vehicles like BitCoin using exchange-traded funds.

Since exchange-traded funds are shares of stock, other than noting what you're investing in, they don't require any special treatment. However, as a swing trader, you can profit handsomely from trading on movements of major indices.

Commodities and Futures Markets

Commodity investing is essentially investing in raw materials. These can be raw materials that can be consumed immediately like pork, or raw materials that are used as inputs to other products such as iron. Natural materials such as oil, natural gas, or uranium – that is energy sources – are also commodities. Metals like gold and silver also fall under this category.

Commodities can change in price wildly over the short-term and so make an attractive alternative for day and swing traders. However, due to the large swings that can result in massive losses of capital, investing in commodities is recommended for advanced traders with a large amount of market experience and isn't recommended for beginner swing traders. That said, how can you invest in commodities?

The most direct way is to buy the material or good in question. Then you could resell it later. To make profits this way, you'd probably have to put up a large amount of capital.

A more convenient way is to invest without having to own the product in question physically. I am sure that you really wouldn't want to fill your garage with copper and then hope that someone comes along to buy it.

One way that you can invest in commodities indirectly is to buy into an exchange-traded fund that tracks commodities. You can go online and look into the various funds that are offered by brokers that have created exchange-traded funds. Two of the biggest ones around are *State Street Spiders (SPDR)* and *iShares*. There are many others, find the ones that appeal most to you. The way you should do this is by studying the past performance of the funds offered by each company.

Exchange traded funds exist for virtually any commodity or sector. You can invest in gold, platinum, or energy, for example. You can also buy commodity stocks. Keep in mind that sometimes direct investments in commodities will outperform commodity funds or stocks, and vice versa. So, it's not an exact analog to owning the commodities and trading in them, but it's close enough for the vast majority of traders, especially beginners.

Another way to invest in commodities is through futures contracts. A futures contract is an agreement to buy or sell a commodity at a fixed price in the future. So you can lock in a price now and then buy or sell at that price later. Obviously, this can have advantages if the price moved the way you thought it would move, but if the price didn't move the way you'd imagined, you could incur huge losses. Of course, many traders are simply trading the futures contracts hoping to make short-term profits. You aren't necessarily going to buy a future contract hoping to buy tons of corn. Of course, farmers will invest in futures contracts for the actual sale of the underlying good. They would do so to lock in what they see as a favorable price as compared to what it might be at harvest time.

Trading in Stocks and Bonds

Most day and swing traders are going to be focused on buying and selling stocks themselves, so investing in Apple, Exxon, Microsoft, Netflix, and so forth. The basic idea here is simple – buy low and sell high. Most of our discussion on swing trading will focus on buying and selling stocks and exchange-traded funds.

You can also engage in bond trading, but most will be focused on stocks. You can even use exchange-traded funds to trade bonds as if they were stocks.

Options Trading

Options are a simple type of derivative contract. In the interests of swing traders, stock market options are what we will concern ourselves with. An option is a contract that allows you to have the right to buy or sell shares of stock in the future at an agreed upon price called the strike price. So in a sense, an option can be like a futures contract. Most options contracts represent 100 shares of stock. The stock that the contract is based on is called the underlying. You can also trade options by writing options contracts, but the focus for swing traders will be buying and selling options on the market over the mid-term. Options can be ideal for swing traders because they require far less capital investment up-front and they have expiration dates over time frames ranging from a week up to two years. Most options that are traded are going to be around a month in duration, which fits in perfectly with swing trading as we will see.

FOREX Trading

Another popular market where investors hope for short-term profits is on foreign exchange. In other words, trading on currencies. This can be very risky but also very lucrative. The billionaire George Soros built a great deal of his wealth using currency trading. Soros made $1 billion by short selling a large amount of British pounds sterling. Although you probably won't make $1 billion, FOREX investing can be very lucrative for small investors. The way FOREX trading works is if you believe one currency x will increase in value relative to another currency y, then you buy x with y. You can then book profits by selling x and converting it back to y. Since the first currency had risen in value (assuming everything worked out for you), then you will have more y than you started with.

Chapter 2: What is Swing Trading?

Swing trading is a short-term strategy that seeks to profit on swings in the value of a stock, commodity, crypto, or the market itself if you are trading index funds. While the phrase short-term is used, this is only relative to long-term investors with time horizons of years to decades. A swing trader is not a day trader and instead looks to profit from changes in market price that occur over days, weeks, and even months. If you are looking to buy a stock and sell it in 6-8 months for a profit, you're a swing trader. If you're looking to buy a stock today and sell it in 3-4 days, you're also a swing trader. A swing trader isn't out to make day trades.

As we will see, it is important to distinguish swing trading from day trading for legal reasons. There are multiple strategies that can be used to both predict market swings and to hedge your bets, that is mitigated or minimize losses. You can swing trade on any market or with any type of asset, including FOREX, gold, or bonds but most swing traders focus on the stock market.

What is Day Trading?

Day trading is considered a high-risk activity and so is heavily regulated. To become a day trader, you must have at least $25,000 cash in your account, and many experts recommend that you have $30,000. Brokerages will strictly monitor who is a day trader and who is not. You can receive a day trading designation by engaging in at least 4-day trades in any 5-day period. To count as a day trade, you must buy or sell the same security more than once on the same day. It's important to understand the rules if you are trading options. You can buy and sell multiple options contracts on the same day without getting the day trade designation if you are trading different contracts. So, if you buy and sell shares of Apple on the same day, that counts as a day trade. But if you buy an options contract on Apple, sell it and buy a different options contract on Apple later in the same day, even though you've made three trades, that does not count for even one day trade.

Day trades carry over the weekend. So if you make your first day trade on Friday, and make a second day trade the following Monday, your day trade count will be 2. If you make 2 more trades by Thursday, then you're going to be designated as a day trader and have restrictions placed on your trading account.

There are some brokerages that don't have the capital requirement, but they take huge commissions. These brokerages are not used by professional day traders but can be used by small investors to learn the art and science of day trading, without having to put up $25,000. Even with the high commissions, if you are good at it — you can make profits.

Day trading relies on several strategies to anticipate moves in the markets. These include various signals that indicate whether a given security is going to increase or decrease in price. If the signal indicates a price increase, that can be a good time to buy. If the signal indicates a coming downturn, that can be a signal to sell your shares. Professional traders don't rely on one signal — they take into account multiple signals to make reasonable bets. Often, the bets will be wrong, and you'll face losses, but people who are skilled day traders are right more often than they are wrong and make substantial profits.

Swing Trading vs. Day Trading

Swing trading is kind of a version of day trading lite. With swing trading, rather than looking to make a profit on moves in a security that occur in one day or less, you're looking to profit on price fluctuations that occur over mid-term time frames. You can think of swing trading as occupying a middle ground in between day trading and conventional stock market investing. Time frames used in swing trading can be as short as 2 days, up to a few weeks, and even out to a few months. You are attempting to capitalize on large moves or swings in the market rather than on short-term moves that a day trader focuses on.

One important distinction is that swing trading is not something that is regulated. There aren't capital requirements placed on swing traders. The only capital that you will need in your account is enough to do the trades that you want to carry out, so you can start small and not worry about putting $25,000 in your account. As far as the brokerage is concerned, if you are not carrying out day trades, you're just another investor.

Since you're not trying to profit on the heat of the moment changes in the direction of a security during a single day, swing trading has a lower risk than day trading. However, the upside is the same. You can profit quite handsomely doing swing trading, probably as much as you can doing day trading. It requires more patience than day trading since you might have to wait several days, or even weeks, or a month before potential profits are realized.

Even so, swing traders use many of the same techniques that day traders use. In some of the analysis a swing trader uses, you will be looking at the same exact signals the day traders are looking at. The only difference will be the time frame of consideration and when you will act on your trades.

While day trading can attract adrenaline junkies who are hoping for quick "wins," swing trading is more suitable for a calm personality looking to build on investments. In both cases, you are hoping for short-term profits that are made-off moves in the securities you invest in. And swing traders also rack up "wins" and "losses." Many times, your trades will be based on assumptions that are simply wrong, and you'll lose money. However, with a less frantic pace, as a swing trader, you'll have more time to carefully consider your trades. Also, you'll have a longer time horizon to realize profits. This can reduce risk because although stocks can plummet fast, they can often recover value given enough time. That won't always happen, but you can see recoveries. There are no hard and fast rules. Unlike a day trade where you will want to exit quickly, you don't have to close your position on a swing trade over any defined time period. You can stay in the position for weeks or months, whatever suits you.

In summary, swing trading is an active form of trading in securities. It will let you take a very active role in the management of your account, and require that you follow financial, economic, and political news very closely to anticipate moves in the securities you are interested in. Also, like day trading, you're hoping to book profits in the near term, rather than buying and holding until you're in retirement.

What Instruments Can You Trade In With Swing Trading?

The answer is basically anything that can be traded. The most frequently used traded securities include:

- Stocks
- Options
- Exchange-traded funds
- FOREX
- Crypto
- Bonds
- Commodities, including gold, silver, and platinum

We will look at each of these in the book and see how to apply swing trading techniques to each particular instrument.

Chapter 3: Market Signals

The bottom line with swing trading is that you're looking to profit from short-term price moves, but the phrase "short-term" is relative. It's short-term relative to the traditional investor. It may be the same as a day trader in some cases, but will typically be a longer time horizon relative to day traders.

While you can swing trade with virtually any instrument, in this chapter we're going to look at market signals used to trade stocks because the same types of market signals used here can be used for virtually any type of investing. Market signals are basically signals that indicate when an upturn or downturn in the price of the security is going to be realized. These signals are not perfect and can never be perfect because markets are chaotic systems, and they are dependent on the emotional states, desires, fears, and logic of thousands of different individuals. Often, people engage in herd behavior and react to the same news in the same way. You might say that the indicators work "most of the time" or at least more often than not. To increase the probabilities that a trade based on a given market signal is right, experienced traders rely on the evaluation of multiple indicators, rather than simply looking at one and declaring the stock is heading up or down and then engaging in the appropriate trade.

Although you need to educate yourself on these indicators and you will use them in swing trading, day trading is more dependent on them. Swing trading is based more on longer-term behavior than it is in a sudden upturn or downturn in a single day or even over a few days. Often, swing trading will rely on events that could include upcoming economic news, the release of a new product, earnings reports, or simply the bullishness investors have for a particular stock. For example, investors are currently bullish on Netflix. Profits can be made by swing trading Netflix in the coming months. A swing trade on Netflix would involve buying shares now, and then preparing to sell them at some point over the next week, or possibly out several months when the share has risen to a point where you can book expected profits. Of course, even though you think Netflix is going to increase over the next few months, you can't *know* if it will do so. Therefore you can incur losses as well as profits. Things may not work out as expected. As a recent example, Apple lost a Supreme Court case related to its exclusive control of the App Store on its iPhones. It remains to be seen how that will work out, but investors hoping the stock will rise may be in for a downward trend instead, as a result of this surprise ruling. This example goes to show that you need to be aware of news events related to stocks that you are trading, not just the latest price to earnings ratios or signals indicating the stock is a good buy.

Candlesticks

The first indicator we will look at has its origins in rice trading in Japan. It's called a candlestick, and candlesticks have applications across a wide range of financial instruments. A candlestick has a body and two wicks, one wick coming out of the top of the body and the other coming out of the bottom of the body. The thickness or height of the body can vary, and the lengths of the restrictive wicks can vary. A candlestick appears as follows:

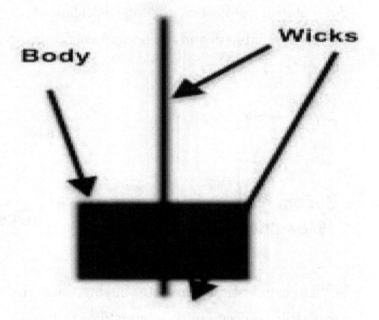

A candlestick tells you the spread of trades and the prices, and whether or not trading is bullish or bearish (meaning traders are buying and driving up the price, or selling off driving the prices down). There are two types of candlesticks. A candlestick will be green on a stock chart (or FOREX or whatever) if it's a bullish candlestick. In that case, the bottom of the candlestick indicates the closing price. This doesn't mean the closing price for the day; it means the price at the end of whatever time period you select for your candlesticks so it can be for 1 minute, 5 minutes, or a day. A day trader is generally going to be interested in looking at charts that show candlesticks for 5-minute intervals. As a swing trader, you'll probably look at daily candlesticks.

For a bullish candlestick, the top wick shows the high price for the time interval and the bottom wick shows the lowest price.

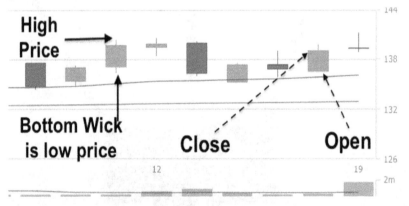

Bullish candlesticks indicate buying, but that doesn't necessarily translate into an immediate uptrend.

A bearish candlestick is red in color on charts. Bearish candlesticks represent traders selling off. Presented on a chart such as a stock chart, since they represent the opposite move to a bullish trade, the top and bottom of the candlestick have the opposite meaning to that found with a bullish candlestick. If the candlestick on your chart is red, the top of the candlestick is the opening share value, and the bottom of the candlestick is the closing value. The wicks still represent high and low prices for the time interval, respectively.

It's important to pay attention to the time interval of your chart so that you understand the meaning of the candlesticks. For example, we can look at a six-month chart for Apple.

In this case, each candlestick represents one day of trading. As a swing trader, this is what you are going to be interested in. You are not looking to make profits by the minute or the hour.

The relative size of the body of a candlestick is a representation of the change in the price of the stock over the course of the trading period represented by the candlestick. A large candlestick body with a changing color can indicate a change in market sentiment. So if there is a green candlestick with a large body, that indicates a lot of traders are buying the stock. The large size of the body indicates that at the close of trading, the price of the stock was a lot higher than at the open. If the candlestick is red in color and has a large body, that indicates that a large number of traders are selling off the stock. In that case, the closing price is a lot lower than the price at the open. Of course, sometimes this is an indication of what is coming next, sometimes it's not.

The important signal regarding the size of the body that traders look for is whether or not it envelops the previous candlestick. That is, you look to see if the candlestick changed in color and if it's larger than the previous candlestick. If so, this is a strong indicator that an upturn (rise in price) will follow if the larger or enveloping candlestick is green, or a downturn is on the way (decline in price) if the latter, enveloping candlestick is red in color. This is what this phenomenon will look like in a chart:

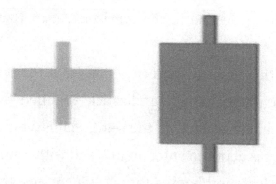

In this case, a small green candlestick is followed by a large red candlestick. This tells us that while a small number of traders briefly bid up the price by buying shares over the time interval to the left, the candlestick on the right indicates a larger and more vigorous sell-off. This probably indicates that a downturn in share price is coming.

That downturn can be an opportunity, so you shouldn't automatically view green as 'good' and red as 'bad.' Buy low and sell high is your motto, so a coming downturn also represents a coming buying opportunity. You can, of course, short the stock but beginning traders are best off learning the ropes profiting in a conventional way.

So let us summarize what to look for when you see two candlesticks next to each other that differ in color. The first case is a green or bullish candlestick followed by a red candlestick, which is bearish. If there is an engulfing pattern, that is the red candlestick is larger than the green candlestick before it, and you see this pattern at the top of an uptrend, this indicates that the stock is going to enter a downtrend or decline in share price. We say that this is a bearish engulfing pattern.

If we see the opposite pattern – that is, at the bottom of a downturn we see a red candlestick engulfed by a green candlestick immediately to the right, that is a bullish signal – the stock is about to enter an uptrend with rising prices.

If you are long and hoping for price increases, then you're looking for bullish indicators. If you are shorting stock or selling put options, then you're looking for bearish indicators.

It's important to recognize that while these are often reliable indicators, they don't work all the time. So you'll need to take other things into account before entering into a trade.

Another indicator to look for with candlesticks is an inverted hammer, sometimes called a shooting star. It looks like this:

Notice that the top wick for an inverted hammer is quite large, while the bottom wick is quite small. That tells us that the price shot up quite high but didn't drop very much. The small body, on the other hand, tells us that the opening and closing share prices were not much different. You will see candlesticks with this pattern at the bottom of downward trends and at the top of upward trends. If it's green and at the bottom of a downward trend, this is an inverted hammer, and it represents a coming upward trend in the share price. On the other hand, a red candlestick with this pattern at the top of an uptrend is a "shooting star," and it indicates a coming drop in share prices.

At the bottom of a downward trend, an inverted hammer is a buy signal if you are hoping the price of the stock (or whatever you are investing in) will rise. As a swing trader, you are going to be looking at buying at the right opportunity, so that you can buy at the lowest possible price and sell at a high price to book profits. This will apply whether you're directly buying stocks or if you are buying call options.

If you are looking to sell, seeing a shooting star at the top of an uptrend is a definite indicator to sell. On the other hand, if you're looking to short the stock or buy put options, then it's a buy signal.

Here is a chart showing a classic shooting star. A downturn in share price immediately follows.

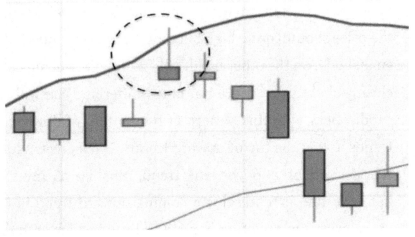

In the chart below, we see an inverted hammer which indicated an upturn.

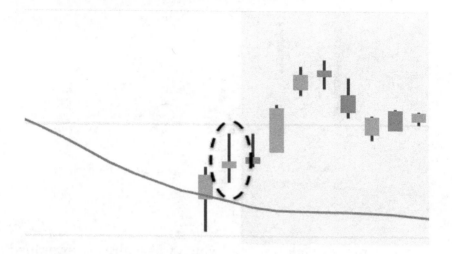

Indecision Candles

A candle that has a small body but large wicks is called an indecision candle. These are also called "spinning tops" or "dojis," and may indicate a coming reversal. What a swing trader will look for is several indecision candles grouped together, which is taken as a stronger indication that a reversal is coming.

Indecision candles are shown here. Note the relatively small body and long wicks emanating from each candle:

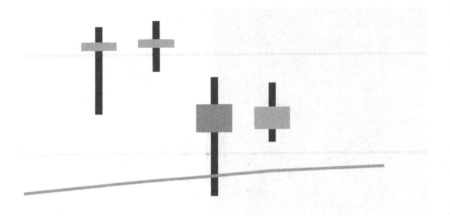

A hammer or shooting star which we've already examined are special types of indecision candles.

Oscillators

The next indicator that we will look at is called an oscillator. You can use oscillators in conjunction with candlesticks for a more solid analysis tools to decide when to buy or sell shares. What an oscillator does is it can compare current market prices to the range of prices over a past period. This indicates the current momentum for the stock or index.

Oscillators are used to search out overbought and oversold assets. If an asset is overbought, that means the price has been driven higher than it really should be, and a coming decline is possible. If an asset is oversold, then an upturn in share price is likely. If you are looking to profit on appreciating stock prices, then you're looking for oversold signals. If you are looking to short a stock, then you're going to look for overbought signals. Oscillators can be utilized when a stock is "moving sideways" or not showing indications that it's going up or down. Moving sideways means that over time, the price of the stock stays within a limited, narrow range.

Oscillators can be important tools to utilize in certain situations, such as when momentum is running out on a trend. For example, consider the 'overbought' situation. As the stock price continues on the uptrend, at some point the volume of trading for the stock will start to decrease, even if the price keeps increasing a little bit. This is a strong indication that interest in the given stock has begun to decrease. In many if not most cases, that can mean that the stock is overbought and selling will begin soon. If you have bought the stock at a lower price, this may be a good time to exit.

Specifically, one tool that you can use to determine when there is an overbought or oversold situation is called the S & P Oscillator Index. One thing this index will tell you is whether the rate of trading is increasing or slowing down. That will give you an idea of what the conviction of the market is on a given stock or index, that is bearish or bullish. You can also utilize the "ultimate oscillator," which relies on three different time frames rather than one-time frame, which is the standard for oscillators.

Like other indicators, oscillators should not be used in isolation. You can use them in conjunction with other tools like candlesticks. Typically, you can look at the candlesticks to get an idea of where they are indicating that the trend is heading. Then you confirm looking at other indicators such as an oscillator. If they all agree, then it's a good time to either enter or exit a trade.

Let's look at the ultimate oscillator on a stock chart. What you want to do is compare the trends shown in the oscillator to the trends in the stock chart for the given security that you are interested in. For the ultimate oscillator, you can pick 7 time periods, 14, and 28 time periods. You will be interested in the following items:

- Buying pressure: This is the closing price minus the minimum price.
- True Range: Maximum – Minimum, where maximum is given by the high price or previous close, and minimum is given by low price or previous close.
- Periods: To get your average periods (say 7 periods), you sum up the seven periods of buying pressure and divide by the 7 periods true range.
- The ultimate oscillator is given by a simple formula that is UO = 100 x (7 Period Average x 4 + 14 period average x 2 + 28 period average)/ (4 + 2 + 1)

You don't need to sit down and do these calculations; this will all be done for you by the computer and displayed by whatever stock chart you are using.

In the example chart below, we show what it looks like when you add the ultimate oscillator to your stock chart. In our case, we used year-to-date values for Apple.

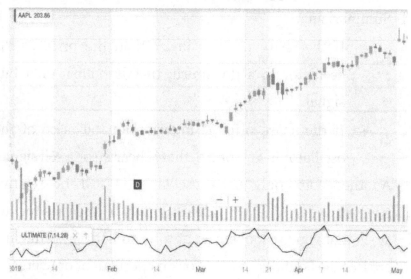

You will compare momentum trends in the oscillator to those in the stock price. Let's look at a buy signal. A buy signal is going to happen during a downward trend. In the case of a buy signal, you are looking for a bullish divergence. This happens when the price of a stock reaches a new low that is lower than the low reached by the oscillator. Traders take this as a signal that bears are losing momentum in the market. So, this is a good time to buy the stock before upward pressure from bulls entering new positions drives the share price up again. A bullish divergence indicates that security is oversold.

Conversely, a sell signal is indicated by a bearish divergence. In this case, the price of the stock forms a high that exceeds that of the indicator. This indicates that the stock is overbought and may soon head into a downward trend.

Summarizing:

- If the share price is lower than the price of the oscillator in a downturn, that is bullish or a buy signal.

- If the share price is higher than the price of the oscillator in an upturn, that is bearish or a sell signal.

Another commonly used oscillator is RSI or relative strength index. The RSI will set up two boundaries for the stock that you are looking at, at top and bottom. If the line crosses the boundaries, the stock is overbought or oversold. Setting this up for apple YTD in 2019, the upper boundary is 80, and the lower boundary is 20. We can see where the chart matches up in trend to the oscillator. In the chart, we have marked to locations where the RSI went past 80, and this corresponded to downturns in the share price.

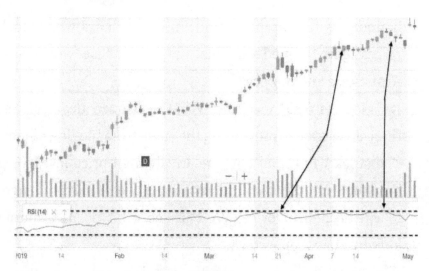

Experienced traders use oscillators to help them determine when the momentum in the market for the security they are interested in is starting to peter out. Generally, oscillators are useful but not considered to be strong indicators. In other words, as a swing trader, you should learn about oscillators in detail and use them in your analysis, but you should not strictly rely on them and only use them in conjunction with other tools.

Support and Resistance

Stock price is not always moving up and down in the large. Since stock prices are chaotic, there are rarely straight lines, the lines are always jagged as the price moves up and down over short-term intervals. However, over extended periods of time, the price fluctuation can become strictly bounded. This happens after a strong upturn or downturn and can indicate a changing sentiment in the market. There are two

47

boundaries that are important in stock charts when stock prices get trapped in this manner; these are called *Resistance* and *Support*.

Let's look at resistance first. What resistance means is that there is resistance preventing the stock from moving higher. The stock will remain at a relatively high price level for a time, but then after bouncing around over a narrow range, it will decline in price. We can see a bit of an example looking at an Apple chart.

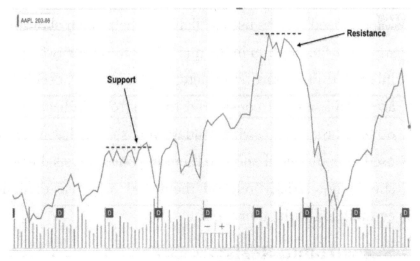

In the section of the chart labeled resistance, the stock never managed to climb above $227.63 a share, although it flirted with the zone from 8/27/18 to 9/24/18, nearly an entire month. As you can see from the chart, there was a massive downturn in the share price. You might take a look at the news at the time, the resistance period may have been the result of either waiting for an earnings report when investors were not certain if Apple would show strong profits, or it could be the result of waiting for the release of the newest iPhone, and perhaps when it was actually released, it disappointed investors.

To summarize, resistance occurs at the end of an upward trend, and then it is indicated by a time period where the stock stays relatively tightly confined by a price range, doing the usual zigzag between higher and lower prices, but never exceeding the resistance boundary. This often indicates a downward trend is coming.

Is a downward trend always coming when you see this signal? Absolutely not. When it comes to the markets, there are always unforeseen events that are out of the control of traders. That can range from natural disasters to unexpected earnings reports. Of course, leaks and rumors will swirl around earnings reports and other news, so there is some idea of what is going on. However, it was always possible that Apple could release unexpected good news, and instead of being a period of resistance, we'd look upon that zone of stagnation as a floor of support. Sometimes support and resistance are only clear after the fact. Support and resistance do indicate a possible reversal, but it might also simply be a "weigh station" on the way to resuming the current trend. That is an illustration of why any given indicator should never be used in isolation.

Which brings us to the other marked section in the chart, where we have indicated a period of support. You can see from the chart that during this time period, the price never managed to get below $169 a share. The time period in the chart is quite long, showing that the share price languished in that zone for 2 months.

Note that when you look at a chart over different time ranges, you may see zones of support and resistance that you didn't notice before. When you look at the chart for one single day, as day traders do, you are going to see a lot more action that results from the chaotic nature of the markets and traders acting as traders do. The key is to look at the chart on time frames that are relevant to the time frames that you are interested in using. If you are a swing trader, then don't look at charts that are broken down into five-minute windows. Also, oftentimes, what you see as support or what you see as resistance can change depending on the time frame and window used to look at the data. When you're looking at support and resistance for the purposes of making a trade, you really have no idea what is going to come next from the future (what doesn't yet exist but would be to the right of where you're currently seeing a sideways move). Just remember, always use multiple indicators to strengthen or perhaps weaken your confidence in making a particular trade.

What Drives Market Momentum

When we are talking about momentum shifts, overbought and oversold securities, what we are really talking about is basic economics. Momentum in the market is driven by the usual supply and demand. A rising share price that hits resistance is encountering dropping demand for that security in the markets. Conversely, when prices drop low enough when the share price has been languishing at a relatively low level, then demand for that security will rise as optimistic traders begin taking advantage of the buying opportunity.

Looking for Uptrends

Sometimes a stock will be locked a longer-term uptrend that means profits can be made by swing traders. Netflix was on such a trend in the first quarter of 2018. Had you got in at the start of the year, you were looking at a solid increase in share price by March.

NFLX 261.30

325.00
300.00
275.00
250.00
225.00

175.00

Often, despite the short-term chaos of the stock market, the security in question is on the path of a definite uptrend or downtrend. You are going to notice this on slightly longer time frames of a few weeks up to a few months. As a beginning swing trader, spotting uptrends is going to be one of your most useful and accessible tools. In the chart above, the share price moved from $201 to $315. You can see from the chart that there was also a countertrend, which was a temporary downturn that occurred in the midst of the overall increase. It's hard to know by simply looking at charts and data whether a downturn is temporary or not. You can significantly up your odds of being correct about future market trends by studying the company (or currency, economy, commodity as the case may be) that you are interested in trading. When you have a nice, relatively smooth and long-term uptrend like Netflix had over the given time period, you could have profited handsomely at nearly any point had you purchased the shares early in the year. Of course, not all of us are so clever or lucky, which is why even the most careful traders sometimes fail to profit or even face losses.

The following illustration indicates what a countertrend looks like in the midst of an overall climb. A countertrend can represent a pullback, which is a direction against the long-term trend.

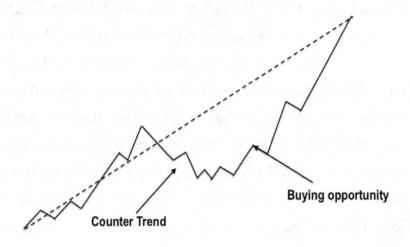

Counter Trend

Buying opportunity

Any point in between the countertrend and the resumption of the upward march would be a buying opportunity, but it would be foolish to buy on one signal alone. One thing you will note is that in between "counter-trend" and "buying opportunity," the stock has basically moved in a sideways fashion, that is you could take the in-between period as support. The stock is unable to dip below a certain low level, which can be an indicator that the upward trend will resume. Moreover, we can look at other signals to either bring more evidence that our view is correct or perhaps to counter it. So, you would be looking at candlesticks, moving averages, and oscillators as well. And you would be reading the latest financial news about the company so that you would enhance your ability to estimate investor sentiment in the coming months.

An aside about this discussion, as a swing trader, "long-term" doesn't necessarily mean over the course of three to five years. Long-term can vary by the situation and be just a few weeks, depending on when you plan to enter and exit a trade. For example, at the time of writing, there is a great deal of uncertainty in the markets. The United States and China have entered into a tit-for-tat trade battle applying tariffs, which has left markets rattled. Nobody knows how long this will last, and even if the tariffs stay in place, nobody knows how long investors will care about it. However, sitting at this point as a swing trader, you have different ways you can approach the market:

- It can be a buying opportunity. Shares are going to be quite a bit lower than they were a few weeks ago, especially for index funds.

- It could be an opportunity to look for more downward movement. A savvy investor might consider buying and selling put options to make short-term profits off the downturn.

None of us are psychic, and even fewer among us have the relevant inside information. So, from where we stand now as a trader, it's virtually impossible to know when the United States and China will reach a mutually satisfactory trade deal if they ever do. It's also impossible to know whether or not the tariffs will really impact the economy. It may be that they aren't high enough to make much difference, and consumers will shrug them off. These are some of the unknowns that an investor would be facing.

Over a short time frame of a week or so, it would be reasonable to bet against the market by investing in put options. This would also be a good way to earn substantial profits on smaller upfront investments.

In this recent chart of SPY, which tracks the S & P 500, we can see some of the candle indicators we've talked about in action. First, note that there was a downturn which had a green (bullish) candle that enveloped the previous red (bearish) candle. That would indicate an upturn, which happened. At the top of the brief upturn, we see a *hanging man*. This is a red, bearish candle that has a high price which never exceeded the open, so there is no wick coming out of the top. There is a long wick coming out the bottom, which tells us that the low price was significantly lower than the closing price. That is a signal of a downward trend, which is exactly what happened. The very end of the data shows a doji, which is green. That could indicate a reversal is coming, but whether or not there is a reversal, that is something that depends on external forces as much as it does on direct investor sentiment at the moment. The news on trade the following day could completely upset the apple cart.

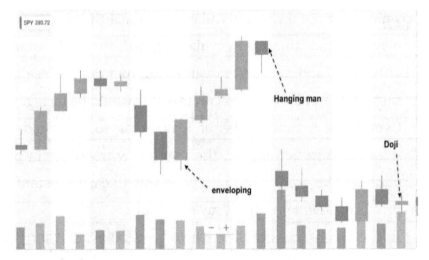

Downtrends

You can take advantage of long-term downtrends as well. There can also be a countertrend during a downturn, which temporarily goes against the grain. There may be bad earnings and other problems that ensure that the stock price will decline for some time. As a swing trader, you don't have to be a victim to the downturn. You can either short the stock, buy and sell puts, or you can even make trades based on short-term signals that result in profits. In order to profit off counter trends, you would look for signals that the stock is about to increase. This will include looking for a period of support, that is coupled with the appearance of reversal or indecision candles. One technique you can use to prevent yourself from suffering from large losses of capital in such trades is to set up a stop-loss order. This is an order to the brokerage to sell your shares if the price goes below a certain value. In the case of support, you can set up a price that is slightly below the support level to use for your stop-loss. Then if the share price drops below that value, your shares will be automatically sold. That will help you avoid a situation that could arise involving a constant drop off in share value as a downward trend is continued.

Flags

So-called flags are other indicators to look for on market charts. A flag is characterized by a sudden shift up in price over a short time period. This is the "flagpole." To form a flag, the price will stay within a narrow range, resulting in a sideways pattern for a time. It could be support, meaning that the stock was ready to resume an upward climb, or it could be resistance, meaning that soon the stock would begin dropping in price. When there is a sudden increase in price over the short term forming a flag pattern, this is called a "bull flag." In many cases, steep increases in share price – caused by a sudden increase in demand – are going to be followed by a stagnant period during which demand becomes more muted, preventing the stock from rising higher. The key indicator for a bull flag is looking for changes in the volume of trading. If it looks like a bull flag on the chart and trading volume went up as well during the steep share price increase, then you know demand is real and more upside is coming. You can buy shares now, entering a stop-loss order slightly below your share price. That way, if your interpretation of the "flag" is mistaken, your losses will be minimal. Setting the stop-loss at a level slightly below your price paid for share ensures that you can get out of the market if it turns into a downturn instead, meaning that the "flag" was actually resistance.

What goes up must come down, and when there is a sudden, steep decline in the market price over a short time period, you might be witnessing a bear flag. After the steep decline, you will see a period of sideways movement when the price sticks to a certain range. This could be a period of support or a brief stop on the way to more declines. If you note high volume trading over the time period of the flagpole, then that is an indicator that it is more likely than not a true flag. This indicates that the downward trend is likely to continue so you can respond appropriately by shorting the stock or investing in put options. Perhaps you've been long on the stock; a bear flag might be a signal to exit the position before you're wiped out.

Whether it's a bear or bull flag, you should look for a signal from some external event that either prompted traders to enter positions quickly or engage in a frantic sell-off. If there is no such external event that can be tied to the security in question, you might not be seeing a true flag pattern.

Moving Averages

Price data can be smoothed out into an average using a tool called a moving average. You can use moving averages with different periods to analyze trends in the market. Averages can be taken over different time periods, like 7 days, 30 days, and so on, giving you a smooth curve that you can see on your market chart along with the price data of the stock of interest. The time frame used for the moving average is referred to as the "lookback period." The shorter the lookback period, the more responsive the moving average will be to price changes, and the more closely it will track the movement of the price.

The first reason to use moving averages is to eliminate noise. The noise comes from the meaningless short-term ups and downs in price that are common in stock charts. A moving average with the appropriate number of periods, can help you establish upward and downward trends, along with overall levels of support and resistance. In other words, imagine the stock price oscillating up and down within envelopes defined by moving averages, with the peaks hitting the resistance and the troughs hitting the support for the stock price. This can be useful for identifying stocks that are in a long-term uptrend that you may want to invest in as a swing trader now, to book profits down the road.

In an upward trend, a 50-day moving average will help you visualize the support level for the stock. In this chart, we show Netflix along with the 50-period moving average.

The shorter the time period you select, the closer the curve will be to the stock price. In this example, we've selected a 10-day moving average. Notice that it's a smoothed-out curve that tracks the stock price.

Stock charts will allow you to add a moving average envelope, which will help you establish a price floor, ceiling, and median. By default, moving averages will use the closing price, but you can also use the open price, high, low, or trading volume.

The chart below illustrates the way that a smaller lookback period will give you a curve that tracks the actual stock price more closely. In the chart, we've added a 5-period moving average that nearly approximates the price changes of the stock, and we've also added a 100-day moving average which you see as the curve that is well below the stock price.

The Rule for Moving Averages

First, take a look at a 20 to a 50-day moving average. If the stock price is above the moving average, then this indicates that the trend is up. In the chart below, we see Tesla. The chart shows two-time frames where this phenomenon can be observed. In the earlier time frame, the trend is up, and the share price is above the moving average. In the time frame that is more recent toward the end of the chart, we see that the moving average is above the share price – that indicates a downward trend, that is clearly visible.

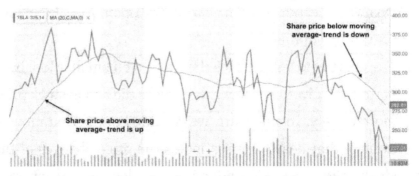

Looking at the chart for the past month, it's really apparent. Notice that at the end of the chart (which is the time that we are writing this book), the moving average is far above the share price. That would indicate that more downward movement is possible.

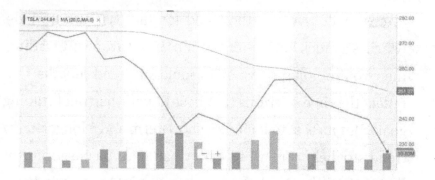

Types of Moving Averages

There are different moving averages that can be used in order to look for different things on your charts. The simplest type of moving average is called the simple moving average, which is nothing more than the average share price at closing (or open, high, low, whatever you select to average). If you create a simple moving average with a period of 20 days, it will simply add up the closing prices and divide by the number of periods. Typically, the closing price is used and that is usually the default provided on most stock charts. While we've been referring to "days," you can create moving averages for any time period you like, so moving averages are often made in reference to "bars," which is going to be the time period represented, so averaging over x-hours, x-minutes, or x-days.

A simple moving average is used to estimate the trend. The more time periods you include in the trend, the longer the "term" of the trend. So, a 5-period moving average will give you the trend for the past 5 periods, while a 100-period

63

average will give you the trend for the past 100 periods, which is a much longer-term trend. If you are swing trading, then you're going to want to look for trend lengths that reflect the time horizons that best fit your personal trading goals. But its best to include a short-term and a longer-term trend, to help you weed out what may be insignificant fluctuations that buck the trend over short time periods.

As we've noted, in the event that the share price is above the moving average, that indicates an upward trend in the stock price. Of course, the stock price can cross the moving average. This is an important signal to look for.

So, if the share price is above the moving average and then crosses below it, that indicates a downward trend. For the swing trader, this might be a signal that you should exit your long positions. Or if you are looking to short the stock, then this can be a time to enter your position.

Vice versa, if the share price is below the moving average and then crosses it, that is an indication that could be a buy signal if you're hoping for rising prices.

You can also look at crossings among the moving averages themselves. In this case, you'll look at short period and long period moving averages together on the same chart. Then, keep an eye out for a moving average crossing the other. This is called "SMA crosses SMA," where SMA means simple moving average. If the shorter period moving average crosses above a long period moving average, that is a buy signal.

If a long period moving average crosses a short period moving average, that is a sell signal.

We can see this for Telsa, on the left side of the chart where the longer-term simple moving average with 50 periods crosses the 20-day simple moving average and remains above it. You can see that subsequent to the crossing, although there was a brief upturn, the stock price has declined since.

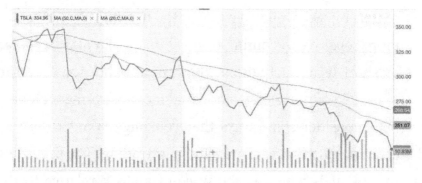

Exponential Moving Average

The simple moving average gives equal weight to all price data. So, if you have a 100-day moving average, the price 100 days ago has the same weight that the price yesterday had. While the price 100 days ago has some relevance, obviously, it is not as influential as the more recent price. The way around this is to use an exponential moving average instead. An exponential moving average gives more weight to recent prices than a simple moving average.

However, an exponential moving average will give you insight into the trend of the stock, so the overall purpose of calculating the moving average is the same. However, an exponential moving average is more sensitive than a simple moving average. Theoretically, this means that it should be able to detect trend changes before a simple moving average will.

There is a downside to this, of course, and it comes from the chaotic nature of stock market data. As we've mentioned many times, stock market data fluctuates up and down quite a bit. So, while an exponential moving average can be more sensitive to coming trend shifts, it can also be fooled by short-term fluctuations. So, you probably don't want to make all your bets on exponential moving averages alone.

Let's consider some ways that you might want to use an exponential moving average in your trading. The first thing to look at is where is the price of a stock relative to the exponential moving average. A rising exponential moving average can indicate an upward trend in the stock price. This can be a buying signal. Then look for a stock price decline. If it goes close to the exponential moving average or better yet falls below it, while the exponential moving average is going up, then that is your signal to buy shares. Conversely, a stock price that gets close to or crosses a declining exponential moving average can be taken as a sell signal.

You can also look for exponential moving averages to indicate zones of support and resistance. If you see something that looks like support in a stock chart, you can confirm this if you see a rising exponential average, which indicates a coming upward trend in the stock price. Conversely, if you suspect you see resistance, this can be confirmed with a downward trending exponential moving average.

Moving averages can be taken together to give a more accurate picture of market trends. If you suspect that an exponential moving average is giving you a false signal, double check with simple moving averages and other indicators such as candles.

When it comes to swing trading vs. day trading, both traders will be interested in both types of moving averages. However, exponential moving averages will gain more interest from day traders, while simple moving averages will gain more interest from swing traders. This is because swing traders have longer time horizons – often much longer, so they won't necessarily want the sensitivity to recent prices that the exponential moving average provides. As a swing trader, you'll also be interested in inoculating yourself against the false signals that the exponential moving average may give you, that result from wild price fluctuations in the recent past. Depending on your time horizon, you will want to use moving averages with longer time periods. Most swing traders use a 50-day simple moving average as their go-to moving average.

Different time periods can also provide different information. You can use the following guidelines to determine what moving average you want to look at for a given type of analysis:

- Use a 20-period moving average when you are looking to spot upward or downward trends.
- Rely mostly on the 50-period moving average. Historical data suggests that it is the most useful indicator when trying to spot a stock that is in an upward or downward trend.
- Use 100-period moving averages to look for support and resistance.
- Always combine your analysis of moving averages with analysis taken from other indicators.

The Golden Cross

Swing traders pay attention to important trading signals that are given by different period moving averages crossing each other. In the following chart of SPY for one year, you will notice that the pink and purple lines cross each other at three points. The pink line represents the short-term or 20-day moving average, and the purple line represents a long-term 100-day moving average.

Notice that when the pink line crosses above the purple line, the price of the stock (in this case SPY) goes up. When a short-term moving average crosses a long-term moving average, we call it a golden cross because it indicates this upward trend in price. This is not too difficult to see why this would be the case, the 20-day moving average is more sensitive to recent trends than the 100-day moving average, so it is certainly more indicative of a change in trend. Often, when looking for a golden cross, a trader will compare the 50-day simple moving average with the 200-day simple moving average. A 200-day moving average gives you quite a long-time horizon covering more than half the year. The bottom line is that if a short-term moving average crosses above a long-term moving average, that is a buy signal if you are hoping for the stock price to go up.

Death Cross

The opposite situation is called a "death cross" and with good reason. When a short-term moving average curve crosses below a long-term moving average, that tells us that share prices are likely to decline. In the graph of SPY above, the signal was painfully accurate. You can see that after a period of moderate support, the share price crashed. Soon afterward, the short-term moving average begins rising until it again crosses the long-term moving average, indicating a new upward trend. A death cross is a sell signal, or if you don't hold a position in the stock, it might be an indication that a buying opportunity is near.

Again, you will want to use a golden or death cross in conjunction with other tools of analysis at your disposal, including simply watching the news to see what is going on that might influence prices. It can be hard to know when the exact best time to buy will be, but zooming in on the downturns lowest point, which occurred on December 26, 2018, we can check the candles for more guidance. At the bottom of the dip, there is a clear bullish envelopment. We have circled this in the chart below.

Looking at other indicators is important. If you bought shares on the day when the enveloping bullish candle appeared, the closing price was $246.18. Had you waited for the moving averages to cross, then you'd have paid $274 per share. The price rose significantly above that level, so you still would have profited but not as much.

It can be instructive to look at the exponential and simple moving averages on the same graph, using the same periods. For this exercise, we'll include two short-term moving averages, the first the same 20-period simple moving average that is already on the graph in pink, and we'll add a green curve which is the 20-period exponential moving average. The first thing to notice is that the exponential moving average tracks the changing stock prices more closely, and on downturns, it crosses the long-term moving average before the simple moving average does so. In this case, it also picks up the new upward trend more strongly than the simple moving average; however, notice that both cross the long-term moving average at the same time.

In the chart, the 20-day exponential moving average is denoted by the green curve.

In this chapter, we have described some of the tools that you can use while swing trading. In the following chapter, we will look at some specific *strategies* used by swing traders.

Chapter 4: 10 Top Swing Trading Strategies

In the last chapter, we've seen many of the tools you can use to estimate when a stock or market index will rise or fall in price. Now, we're going to look at different strategies used by professional swing traders that will help a trader make more profitable trades. The strategies are not mutually exclusive. You aren't necessarily going to stick to one trading strategy all the time. The tools and indicators in the last chapter can be used by virtually anyone, no matter their trading strategy. The indicators are there to help you determine the direction of the market or the specific investment that you are interested in.

Trendline Trading Strategy

Trendlines can tell us which direction a market is going (stocks, FOREX, crypto, etc.). Trendlines can be used as a trading strategy by themselves, or in conjunction with other trading strategies. An important use of trendlines is to help a trader avoid being fooled by a market pullback that occurs amid a larger trend. When pullback ends, the long-term trend will resume.

Trendlines can be drawn on charts. The purpose of drawing a trendline is to determine where future lows will occur. If there is an upward trend, you can draw your trendline in the

73

following way. First, look for price peaks and lows in the market data. In the case of an upward trend in price, you will focus on drawing your trendlines between one low point in price to the next. So, start by looking for the first low of interest toward the left-hand side of the chart. Draw the trendline from that low to the next low point in price. Then extend it out past the right of the chart so that you can get an idea of where the next low point will occur.

When there is a downward trend in the market, you can also draw trendlines, but you connect high points in the waves instead of lows. Start your trendline at the first highpoint of the price and draw the trend to the next highpoint. Then you can continue to draw the trendline out past the right to estimate where the next high point will occur.

You should draw your trendlines connecting at least two peaks or lows in price. If you can connect more, the trendline will be more accurate.

You don't have to draw trendlines with pencil and paper; online stock charts are set up so that you can draw trendlines on them while on your computer. In the example below, we have added a trendline for the downturn in Netflix price. The two arrows indicate the two peaks that were used to draw our trendline. Notice that the trendline sets a boundary that the price of the stock doesn't cross until the underlying trend reverses.

The purpose of drawing trendlines is to determine support and resistance price levels. While we've illustrated this with a trendline connecting two peaks, notice that it follows the real trend of the stock price very nicely. However, trendlines don't always work so neatly, and we see in the same chart that once the uptrend began, the trendline drawn between the first two lows doesn't produce much as far as future accuracy. Quite soon it overshot actual prices by a large margin.

What this error indicates is that you should not use trendline trading by itself any more than you would do so with other methods or indicators.

Floor Trader Method

The floor trader method has proven to be very useful for FOREX trading but can be used no matter what market is in your interest. This type of method requires the use of moving averages, which we discussed extensively in the previous chapter. Simply put, the floor trader method uses the two moving averages to identify the trend. Then you trade in the direction of the trend. This method relies on pullback or retracements as they are referred to in FOREX. In the midst of a major price trend, a retracement is a temporary pullback in the other direction. A retracement differs from a reversal in that it's a temporary aberration taking place within that larger trend, while a reversal is an actual change in the direction of the trend. The floor trader method has many rules that you can follow depending on what your investment goals are. Let's start by looking at the case where you're looking for the price of the instrument to rise, such as a rising stock price.

To use this method, you'll use two moving averages, a 9-period exponential moving average, and an 18-period exponential moving average.

An uptrend is indicated when the 9-period exponential moving average crosses the 18-period moving average and rises above it. In the chart below, the blue moving average is the 18-period moving average, while the purple line represents the 9-period moving average. Note the two circled points where this type of crossing occurred and the subsequent uptrends.

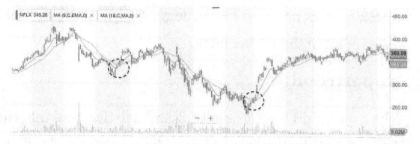

Retracements are lows that occur against the overall upward trend. Traders are advised to wait until a retracement occurs to enter a position. The low price should touch the 9-period moving average or even both moving averages. Then you buy when you see a reversal candlestick that could indicate that the major trend is resuming. You can put a stop-loss order 1-5 pips below the low price point of the retracement.

The floor trader's method can also be used to short the stock on a downtrend. In this case, a downtrend is indicated by the 18-period exponential moving average. In the Netflix chart above, you can clearly see that the blue line, which is the 18-period exponential moving average, corresponds to downward trends very nicely when it is above the 9-period moving average. A crossing of 18 above 9 indicates the downward trend, and then you will wait for the retracement. This is noted when the price reverses (temporarily) and touches or comes close to the 18-period exponential moving average. To short the stock, sell when you see the candlestick indicate that the main trend is going to resume.

Forex traders put stop-loss orders 1-5 pips above the peak price point of the retracement.

Supertrend

The supertrend indicator is another analytical tool that can be used to identify upward and downward trends in the market. A supertrend indicator is defined by the period and by a multiplier. The typical values used for these are a period of 7 and a multiplier of 3.

Online market charts will allow you to overlay a supertrend onto the price chart for the stock or other investment you are interested in. When the supertrend falls below the share price, this is a buy indicator. This will be shown as a green line on the chart. Of course, this is assuming that you are interested in a rising price for the asset.

A red line on the chart occurs when the supertrend is above the share price. In that case, it is a sell indicator. On the supertrend, a sell indicator or red line tracks a downward trend in prices, while a green or buy indicator tracks an upward trend quite nicely. In the following chart, we show the supertrend indicator together with Netflix stock.

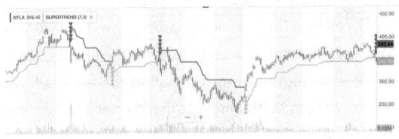

Gartley

The Gartley pattern is also known as "ABCD." This was developed by a trader named Gartley in 1935. It has four-letter designations because you seek out a pattern that has four price swings. The Gartley pattern can be used in any kind of market. The pattern can be used for a bullish or a bearish strategy if you know what to look for. The pattern will include an overall trend and a retracement. Let's first look at an ABCD chart, which is a buy signal.

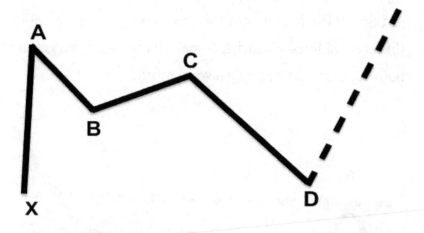

From point X to point A, we see the upward trend. The goal is to trade with the long-term trend. A Gartley pattern will have some sort of "M" shape in the chart. You can see from our fictitious example that there is an M that looks somewhat distorted. The dashed line is not part of the Gartley pattern, but instead is a continuation of the upward trend. The best point to buy is at the bottom of the retracement, which would be point D. You can use other indicators to estimate where this point will be, such as looking at candles and moving averages.

You can draw Fibonacci levels on your chart to estimate how far a price will move after the completion of a pullback. This will help you determine profit targets when attempting to trend with the trade. Fibonacci levels don't require a math degree to calculate; in fact, you pick three points on the chart and have the computer do it for you. However, typical values are 61.8%, 100%, 138.2%, 161.8%, 200%, and 261.8%. If the four legs of the chart end up at a high point, this is considered a bearish signal. Of course, if you get in at point C, then you've made a solid profit.

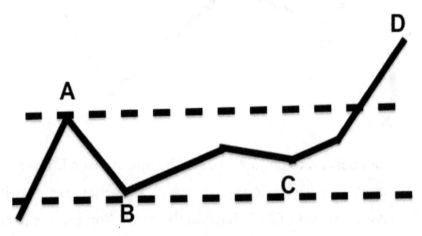

In the above chart, the line B-C is a retracement. Point B indicates the support level. The trader should look at other indicators to confirm what the pattern demonstrates.

Bollinger Bands and Dynamic Support and Resistance

A Bollinger band is an envelope around the prices in a market chart. The main point of Bollinger bands is to identify levels of support and resistance, that is price levels below which the stock is unlikely drop below or that the stock is unlikely to go above. Bollinger bands provide more in-depth information than you can get from trend lines or moving averages by themselves. There are three things that we can get information about by using Bollinger bands. First, we will see two trend lines. A trend line below the market price will indicate the level of support. There will also be a trend line above the market price, which tells us the level of resistance. These are dynamic in that they change with the market price as time goes on. The second thing that Bollinger bands will inform us about is the volatility of the stock. Volatility is simply a measure of how much the price moves up and down over a given time period and how big the price swings are. If you think of a really jagged stock chart with big highs and lows, that is a stock with high volatility. A smooth curve that increases slowly would be an example of low volatility. Finally, Bollinger bands, by providing an envelope around the price curve, tell us the extent to which prices are varying.

Using Bollinger bands requires a moving average. In the Netflix chart below, we've added Bollinger bands with a 20-day moving average. What the Bollinger bands tell us is how the prices spread about that moving average.

Using a different moving average will produce different Bollinger bands. With a longer moving average, you'll expect to see more fluctuation. This is because what the Bollinger bands represent in a mathematical sense is the standard deviation about the moving average. Over a longer time period, the stock has more chance to change in value by larger magnitudes. Below we show the Bollinger bands using a 50-day moving average. You can compare that to the 20-day moving average in the above chart.

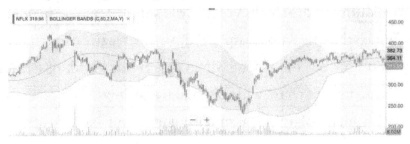

Notice that the bands are much wider and at a few points the price of the stock goes outside the Bollinger bands.

Now, let us consider all things being equal, so focus on Bollinger bands with a 20-day moving average. Wide Bollinger bands indicate more volatility in the market price of the stock. Narrow Bollinger bands indicate less volatility. This makes sense, with more variation in the price you would expect a larger standard deviation (by default charts will show two standard deviations).

Bollinger bands are used to weed out buy and sell signals from the trend. They can also be used to determine whether the stock is currently priced too high or low. When the stock price is at the moving average, the middle line in between the Bollinger bands, it's considered neither priced too high nor priced too low.

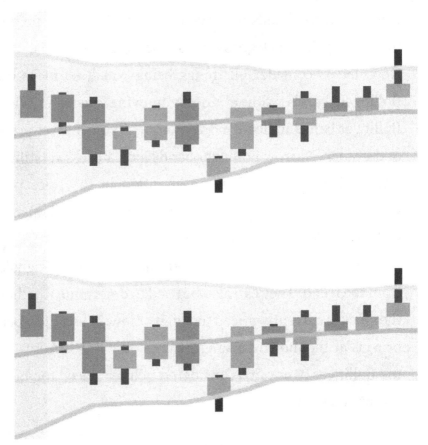

Now consider when stock prices touch the top of the Bollinger bands or even lie outside. In that case, the stock is judged to be overpriced. This is shown below when the stock price is rising.

Now let's consider the opposite situation. When the stock price is near the bottom of the Bollinger bands, or possibly falling below it, that is a cheap-priced stock.

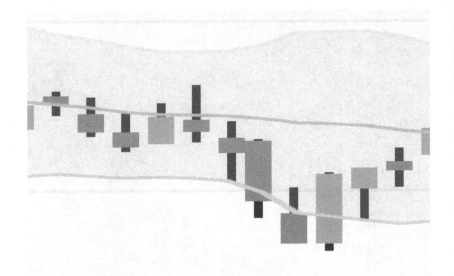

So, you can use Bollinger bands to get buy and sell signals. You can also look at the wicks of the candlesticks and their relation to the Bollinger bands. If you are in the middle of a downturn, an oversold stock can be indicated when the wicks are touching the bottom of the Bollinger band, or falling just outside of it. An overbought stock will be indicated by the opposite, that is, look for the wicks of the candlesticks to touch or go outside the top Bollinger band. If you get an oversold signal from the Bollinger bands, that is a buy signal if you are looking to belong on the stock. If you get an overbought signal, you're going to be interested in selling the stock and booking your profits.

You can also look for reversal signals in Bollinger bands. If the entire body of a candlestick moves outside a Bollinger band, this may be a reversal signal.

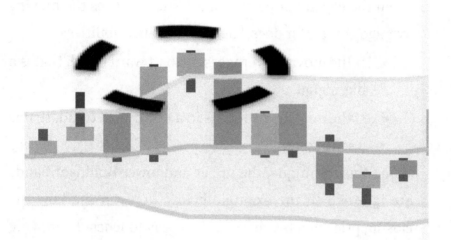

In a downturn, look for a hammer. A hammer in a downturn may be an indication of a trend reversal which will swing into the uptrend. At the top of an uptrend, a shooting star touching the upper Bollinger band can be an indicator of a coming downtrend.

Like any tool, a Bollinger band is not perfect and won't be right all the time. You should use the information you gather from Bollinger bands in conjunction with other indicators.

Middle Bollinger Band FOREX Trading Strategy

This strategy is popular in FOREX markets. In this strategy, the focus is on the midline in the Bollinger bands, which is the moving average curve. Use a 20-period moving average and two standard deviations. You want to look for points when the closing price of a candlestick touches the moving average curve. If it does, there are two possibilities:

- If the moving average is in an upward trend, that is a buy signal.
- If the moving average is in a downward trend, that is a sell signal.

Using this technique, the upper and lower Bollinger bands are ignored. In the example below, you can see how the closing price of a bearish candle nearly touches the moving average or middle curve in the Bollinger bands. That can be used as a selling signal. The moving average curve at that point has a downward slope. Notice the downward trend continues after that point.

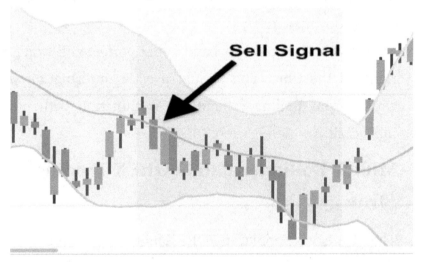

CCI Moving Average Forex Trading Strategy

With this strategy, which is used in FOREX trading, you use the CCI oscillator. CCI can tell you if the trade that you are looking at is overbought or oversold. The oscillator is used in conjunction with the moving average in order to establish a trend.

This strategy requires the use of two moving averages. The first moving average to use is a 7-period Exponential moving average. It should be used in conjunction with a 14-period exponential moving average. You will look for crossovers between the moving averages.

When the 7-period EMA crosses over the 14-period EMA to the upside, that is a setup for a buy signal. To ensure that the retracement is not a reversal, wait for the price to return to the moving average. If the CCI oscillator is below 100, then this is the time to buy. You can also look for bullish candlesticks prior to buying.

Your selling strategy relies on the 7-period EMA crossing over the 14-period EMA to the downside. Prices will drop, but you'll want to wait for them to move back to the moving average. When the CCI goes above 100, that is a sell signal.

Picking Tops and Bottoms Trading Strategy Using ADX Indicator

This is another FOREX trading strategy. ADX is an average directional index. This not only indicates trend direction but also how strong the trend is. Tops and bottoms indicate that we are looking for points on the price curve that are maximums and minimums before a reversal. In the case of a top, what this means is that a bullish or upward trending price curve is about to top out, indicating that a selling strategy would be appropriate. In the case of a bottom, this means that a downward or bearish trend is about to reach its low point so this could be a buying opportunity.

In other words, we are about to hit a reversal.

Two moving averages are used with this strategy. These are the 20-period exponential moving average and the 40-period exponential moving average. For the ADX trend indicator, use the default value of 14 periods.

In this strategy, the 20-period exponential moving average is used to determine support and resistance. The ADX indicator is used to find points of reversal. When the ADX tops 30, this is a sign that there is a strong trend. At any point, you want to look at crossings between the two moving averages. You're looking for the 20-period exponential moving average to cross the 40-period moving average to the upside or the downside, which represent buying and selling opportunities, respectively.

If a candlestick touches the 20-period exponential moving average after it crossed to the upside of the 40-period moving average, this is a buy signal. The lower moving average, which is in this case, the 40-period exponential moving average can be used as a guide for stop-loss orders. They should be placed 2 pips below that line.

Now, consider the case of the 20-period exponential moving average crossing to the downside of the 40-period moving average. This can be taken as a selling signal. Again, you'll look for a candlestick to touch the 20-period line.

Both strategies should be employed only when the ADX tops 30 so that you're sure of trend strength.

The Hull Moving Average

The Hull moving average was developed to eliminate price lag. You can use a 50-period Hull moving average to indicate a trend. You will find that it fits pricing data very nicely. In the chart below, we show the Hull moving average as the purple line laid over Netflix pricing data.

When the Hull Moving averages turn upward, this can be taken as an entry signal to enter a long position. Likewise, downturns in the Hull moving average curve suggest entering a short position.

You can also use Hull moving averages with two different periods. On Forex markets, it is common to use 7-period Hull moving averages and 14-period Hull moving averages and to look for the 7-period moving average to cross the 14-period moving average.

Crossing to the upside indicates an upward trend while crossing to the downside indicates a downward trend.

In this chart, you can see how accurate the Hull moving average can be. This is an overlay of the 7-period Hull moving average over the price data. It tracks it nearly exactly.

In the chart below, notice the purple line, which is the 7-period Hull moving average, and the blue line, which is the 14-period Hull moving average. Soon after the crossing, you see a strong uptrend. Near the top of the uptrend, the 7-period Hull moving average crosses below the 14-period moving average. Although the share price still went up, the continued uptrend was brief and followed by a downtrend. Another crossing quickly resulted in another uptrend.

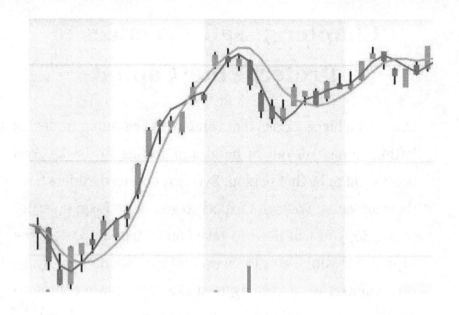

Chapter 5: Safe Practices to Protect Your Capital

One of the biggest risks that come with beginning traders is letting things get out of hand and ending up broke. You don't want to be that person. Even experienced traders have their losses, so you can't expect to go out and win on every trade. So, you will need to take some steps to protect the capital that you're able to invest and live for another day. In this chapter, we are going to make some basic common-sense suggestions that every trader should take to heart.

It can be tempting to bet the farm when you see a "sure thing." The problem is that throughout the history of markets, from the very first tulip craze to the present day, too many people have seen a sure thing and ended up broke. Despite all the signals and indicators that we've discussed in this book, they can often point in the wrong direction. Swing trading isn't rocket science — it's more like a middle ground between art and science. The reality is that unexpected events can derail even the best indicators. We mentioned this earlier in the book – a recent demonstration of this was given when President Trump simply put out a tweet threatening tariffs on China. Whether you think there should be new tariffs on China or not is completely beside the point. For our purposes, we want to learn the lesson that this episode provides for traders. The day before the tweet, the markets were enjoying a massive rally. He sent the tweet out on Saturday. First thing Monday morning, the markets tanked. Had you invested in your sure thing that Friday before, you would have been wiped out in one day. The point of all this is events that are unforeseen happen all the time. What Trump tweeted on Saturday had nothing to do with what the moving averages and candlesticks were doing on Friday at closing.

Even without tweets, earthquakes, and wars, when all the indicators are pointing in the right direction, you can still end up with a loss. The reason is that even though the markets do display some level of order and you can use signals to anticipate reversals and uptrends, underneath it all the market is still a chaotic system that depends on the actions of thousands of individuals.

Only risk 1% of your capital on a trade

With that in mind, we can get to some commonsense approaches that will help keep your losses in check. The first rule is to limit the amount of capital from your trading account that you risk on each trade. At first glance, the 1% rule seems awfully conservative. You might think that you'll never be able to execute a single trade. But that's not the case. The 1% rule is about your actual risk of loss. You can manage your risk of loss with what's known as a stop-loss

95

order. A stop loss order can be placed when you buy your shares (as an example), and it will tell the broker to sell your shares if the price drops to a certain level. So, if you buy shares of XYZ for $45 a share, you can put a stop loss order of $44 a share. If XYZ tanks, then you're only out $1 a share because when the stock hits $44 on the way down, your shares will be sold automatically. If you bought 100 shares, then you're out $100, just $1 a share. If you hadn't bought the stop-loss order and for some reason, XYZ drops to $20 a share, you'd be out $25 a share instead, which would be $2,500.

Now consider another example, suppose that you had a $50,000 account. Now, 1% of $50,000 is just $500. If we are willing to risk $0.25 a share on a trade, that will allow us to buy 2,000 shares. So, if AAA is trading at $20, then we put a stop-loss order at $19.75.

Of course, limiting your risk this way isn't the only way to go. It all depends on how disciplined you are and if you let short-term emotions get the best of you. New traders starting out may not have a taste for the 1% rule because they can only put $1,000 in their account, say. That would only allow you to risk $10, which puts you in a position of not really being able to trade anything.

Another path that you can take is to simply put the amount you can afford to lose into your trading account and nothing more. In the beginning, you should think of your swing trading account as a kind of a hobby with a limited budget until you learn the ropes. If you can afford to lose $4,000 without getting into financial troubles, then that can be a reasonable amount of money to risk. On the other hand, if you put in $25,000 and losing it would mean losing all the money that you had, that would be a bad move. Sit down carefully and evaluate the amount of money you can risk and still pay your rent/mortgage, buy food, and keep your utilities on.

Stop-Loss Orders

As we mentioned above, every trader should use stop-loss orders. You can use a stop-loss order to make sure you sell a declining asset if any further declines would make your losses intolerable. It's important not to get too paranoid about losses as a swing trader, but you need to apply common sense. The specific values you're willing to accept will depend on your personal situation and vary from trader to trader. However, we can make a note – swing trading is not day trading. Why is that important? Because a longer time horizon often gives ample opportunity for reversals. You can be a swing trader and set your own time horizon, but you don't have to close your positions in a day. So, in many cases, it may be appropriate to allow yourself to take a loss knowing that often, the loss will be temporary, or at least it will not be as great as seems initially. Of course, this isn't always true; you'll have to evaluate each real-world scenario on its own merits. Some stocks that crash are not going to recover. It's going to depend on many factors, such as the reasons behind the crash. Did the stock crash because of some event that happened to the company? For example, shares of Bayer crashed to seven-year lows when a jury awarded $2 billion in a suit over the weed killer called Roundup. Whether or not Roundup causes cancer – it probably doesn't – or whether or not a $2 billion judgment is reasonable, are beside the point. Events like that scare off investors. If you had invested in Bayer stock, in that case holding onto it looking for an upswing is probably a bad idea. The pattern of lawsuits suggests that Bayer is going to have to make more payouts or worse.

In other cases, temporary setbacks may be just that. Whether you can live with a temporary setback also depends on how long you're willing to hold onto the stock. Are you willing to wait 9 months for an uptrend so you can exit with a profit? If not, then you should get out now and accept your losses.

Have preset profits in mind

One problem that plagues beginner investors is not having rules for the kinds of profits they will take. If you don't have a rule, then you're always going to be hoping for continual upward trends. You'll be hunched over your computer looking for reversals and gains that never come after it reaches the top and crashes down.

The thing to remember is upturns never last forever. So, you need to set specific exit criteria and stand by them. For example, some people set a gain of 10% in stock price as their goal. If they have a long position and the share price rises 10%, then they sell their shares no matter what. You might have a specific dollar amount in mind. When trading options contracts, you could set a rule that you'll sell and book your profits when the profit reaches $50 per option contract.

It doesn't matter what the details are as far as your rule, as long as a rule isn't unrealistic, and you stick by the rule no matter what. You are going to miss out on some opportunities and not make as much money as you could have. However, more often than not, what you're going to be doing is protecting yourself from losses. The bottom line is that many people hold on too long, hoping to make another $1 in profit, and end up losing everything instead.

One way to handle this is to enforce discipline by having the market take care of this for you. This can be done using a sell limit order. A sell limit order will only go into effect if the price of the asset is at or above the price specified in the limit order. So, if you buy shares in Netflix and decide to sell them when the price reaches $380, then you can put a sell limit order in with that price. If the stock rises to $379 and drops down, it won't be triggered. If it rises to any price at or above $380, then the order will be triggered, and your shares will be sold automatically, crediting your account with the proceeds. For a swing trader, having such protection in place makes sense. It will keep you from making predictable but disastrous mistakes.

Diversify your investments

You might be surprised to see this one in a book about swing trading. Diversifying your portfolio is normally something done by boring people looking to build an IRA.

However, this applies to swing traders as well. You should never put all your eggs in one basket. In the beginning, you may have to do your swing trading on the side for a while before you start making an income from it. You may only be able to concentrate on trading a few securities, but if you can afford it, you should expand your trading activities so that you're not dependent on one stock or two. You can also trade in multiple markets. There is no reason not to at least look at getting involved in bond markets, options trading, or newer markets like crypto. Of course, that will all depend on how much time you have to devote to study. If you feel you don't have the time to push into multiple investment markets, then at least look at doing more than one trade in the market you choose to be involved with.

Chapter 6: Swing Trading Cryptocurrency

In the past decade, one of the newest trading markets to take shape in the world is so-called cryptocurrency like bitcoin. Let's explore how to go about trading crypto in this chapter.

Finding an exchange

The first problem that crops up with crypto is the fact that it's had kind of a mysterious black hat reputation. That still carries on today even though trading crypto is becoming more mainstream. One way to trade crypto that is guaranteed legit is by using the smartphone brokerage called Robinhood. It allows you to trade bitcoin and litecoin. Some of the largest and legit crypto exchanges that specialize in it include Gemini.com, primexbt.com, and Coinbase. Also, you should note that exchange rates can differ from exchange to exchange for the same cryptocurrencies.

Experts in the area also recommend that you only deal with sites that require government issued ID. Since this is still a new area, it is a bit of the "wild west," and trading crypto can be risky if you're not careful.

Actually managing cryptocurrency

There are many different coins that can be traded. The coins are stored in a virtual wallet. It requires a public address and a private key, just like any encrypted computer system. The wallet can store the coins, and it can also receive coins or be used to pay them out. The public address is given out to others so you can exchange coins with them. The private key allows you to send, receive, and access cryptocoins. It should never be given out to anyone.

If your wallet is connected to the internet, it is said to be a type of "hot storage." Any hot storage provides ready access to cryptocurrency. Hot wallets allow quick access but can be vulnerable to hacking. The wallet will be stored on a device like your computer, so you should backup important info like private keys in case something happens to your computer, including having it get stolen.

You can have a wallet on the exchange, or a mobile or desktop wallet. For extra security, you can get a wallet that has multiple signatures.

You can also store cryptocurrency in "cold storage". This is like putting it in a bank vault, you will have less ready access to it, but it is going to be less vulnerable to hacking and theft. Cold storage wallets are cut off from the internet, so there is not any danger of hacking and so on. Crypto stored in cold storage is not readily available for daily transactions.

However, a popular way to use cold storage that can be quickly accessed is to use a USB stick for cold storage. That way, you can connect it or remove it from internet access by connecting it to your computer or not. Special USB sticks made by a company called Ledger have to be used for this purpose. Alternatively, you can use a device called Trezor.

You can actually print out your keys and a QR code on a piece of paper to create what's called a paper wallet. While this keeps your crypto out of reach of the computer, it also puts up additional barriers to accessing your coins quickly. If you are going to be a trader, then this is probably not the option for you.

Trading on an Exchange

Finance is the most popular exchange for trading. Many sites only allow you to purchase cryptocurrency with your government issued money. Keep in mind that you may need bitcoin to start trading on an exchange.

Just like on other markets, trading bitcoin will require you to pay commissions and fees. Familiarize yourself with what those expenses are for the exchange that you select.

Once you've got your cryptocurrency, then you're all ready to go. After that, trading crypto is no different than trading anything else, the same indicators and charts are used, and you can use all the techniques discussed in this book to trade crypto.

Trading using Robinhood

If you have a smartphone, using Robinhood may be one of the easiest ways to get into trading crypto. You can also trade stocks and options using Robinhood. Please see the appropriate App Store for more information.

Chapter 7: Options Trading

Options trading is fast becoming one of the most popular ways to get into trading on the stock market. Since options come with a built-in expiration date, they are almost designed for swing trading. Trading options requires lower amounts of upfront capital and can provide huge ROI as compared to trading stocks. Keep in mind that like any other type of investing, trading options carry some risk.

What is an Option?

Many people aren't clear what an option is. First and foremost, it's a derivative contract. A derivative contract has a value that is based on some other asset. In this case, that other asset is 100 shares of stock. Now, why would it have value? This is because an option gives you the right to buy or sell the shares of stock. Many people find this appealing because options are priced at levels far lower than the stock that underlies the option contract. This allows traders to control large numbers of shares while putting up far less investment capital.

There are two basic types of options, depending on whether you are long or short on the underlying security. A call option is an option that you would buy if you are bullish on the underlying stock.

A call option gives you the right, but not the obligation, to buy 100 shares of stock at a pre-determined price. That price is called the strike price. For example, if you wanted to invest in XYZ and it was trading at $100 a share, you could buy an option contract on XYZ with a strike price of $102. You will do this if you think that the price of XYZ is going to increase in the near future. That is, you would be bullish on XYZ.

When a call option is priced so that the strike price is higher than the trading price, it's said to be out of the money. The reason is there isn't any real advantage to owning the option. You could buy the shares on the open market, but if you exercise your rights under the option, you would have to buy the shares for $2 more per share. That doesn't make sense – until you start considering that stock prices are always changing. If the stock price goes above $102, then the option is said to be in the money. The reason is the option now has a lot of value since it would allow you to purchase shares of XYZ at a lower price than they are trading for on the market. The pre-arranged price is called the strike price.

There is a catch. The catch is that options come with an expiration date. And the closer they get to the expiration date, the less value they have. Trading options successfully generally means knowing how to hedge your risk and paying close attention to the expiration date.

The fact is most options aren't ever exercised. That is, even though call options give you the rights to buy shares of stock, the vast majority of options traders never do. Instead, they buy and sell (that is trade) the options until they expire, looking to make profits off of price movements of the stock. Generally speaking, for every $1 increase in the price of the underlying stock, the price of the option will go up by around $0.50-$1 per share. Since the option controls 100 shares, that means that the option will be going up to $50 to $100 in price. The closer you get to expiration and the more the stock goes up above the strike price, the closer it will get to changing at $1 a share. But there is a constant battle with options between rising stock prices and the closing time to expiration.

If an option is in the money, you can sell it for a large profit. At the time of writing, a call option on Amazon that expires in 2 weeks that has a strike price that is just $1 above the share price is trading for $42. That is a per share quote, and an option controls 100 shares. So, the option will cost $4,200. If Amazon goes up by $100 a share – not impossible by any means relative to its current price – you could expect the option to go up in price to well over $10,000.

Even cheap options contracts can be lucrative. For example, you can invest in SPY, an exchange-traded fund that tracks the S & P 500. These options are priced at much lower levels than Amazon, allowing you to buy contracts anywhere from $50 to a few hundred dollars. It's possible to double your money easily using options for index funds, as a one or two dollar increase in the underlying security can cause the price of the option to go up by $50-$200. You can then sell the option and take your profits.

Put Options

Of course, we don't want to paint a false picture. As recent news has shown, stocks can decline in value as fast or faster than they rise. So, earnings on options aren't automatic. If the gains don't materialize and the option expires with a share price that is higher than the strike price for the call option, it expires worthless. In that case, you're out the premium you paid for the option. Compared to shares of stock, the premium paid will be quite a bit lower. While the option for Amazon stock would cost $4,200 to control 100 shares, actually buying the shares would cost $183,500.

One of the most intriguing features of options contracts is that you can easily bet on market downturns using put options. It is just easier to buy put options than it is to short stock. A put option gives you the right to sell 100 shares of stock at the strike price. Suppose that XYZ is trading at $100 a share. If you buy a put option with a strike price of $90, if the share price drops to $30, the writer of the put option would be obligated to buy the shares from you at

$90. So, you could buy them for $30 on the market and turn around sell them to the writer of the put option and book $60 in profit per share.

But like call options, put options are rarely exercised. Instead, they are traded for profits, and most are allowed to expire. You can trade options to make profits off of downturns. If the share price drops, the price of a put option rises.

Maximum Losses

The maximum losses that you can incur buying options contracts are the price paid for the option, which is called the premium. So, your losses are limited by definition. Gains, on the other hand, are theoretically limitless. Of course, it doesn't work like that in reality, but potential profits far outstrip maximum losses. You can always sell an option at a lower price if it's not working out for you to avoid losing the entire premium. You can use loss limiting techniques that you can use in any other trading, including stop-loss orders and sell limit orders.

Tools to Use Trading Options

Options are temporary. So, by their very nature, they are suitable to day and swing trading. Long-term investors who like to play it safe and have a financial manager or invest in mutual funds are by definition, not going to have much interest in trading options.

The same indicators and tools can be used to evaluate your options trades. However, you won't be applying them to the options themselves, but rather to the underlying stock. You can also access an options calculator from tastytrades.com, search for options data science. The calculator will automate pricing estimates for the option. You just enter in basic data like the current share price, days to expiration, and the strike price for the option. It will take into account the loss in value from closing time to expiration for you and estimate your profits.

When are Options Out of the Money?

A call option is out of the money when the strike price is above the share price. The breakeven point is when the strike price + price paid for the option (per share) is equal to the share price. An out of the money option is worth nothing once time runs out on the option. If the strike price of a call option is below the share price, then the call option is in the money and can be sold at a profit, or you could exercise your rights under the options contract and buy the shares if desired. Some people actually do this if they actually want to own the particular shares of stock in question.

Put options work in the opposite direction. So, a put option is out of the money when the share price is higher than the strike price. The breakeven point is calculated by subtracting the cost of the option from the strike price. If the share price goes below the strike price, then the put option is in the money. It's in the money because you could buy cheap shares on the market and sell them for a profit at the strike price.

Time Horizons for Options

The main factor with time horizons for options is the expiration date. You can purchase options that expire on multiple expiration dates, including some that only last for one week. Options usually expire on Wednesdays and Fridays, and when you look to trade options, you can find options that expire on multiple upcoming dates, some in the current week and others going all the way out for several months. The longer the time to expiration, the more expensive the option. LEAPS are long-term options that last 2 years.

A Good Way to Learn Swing Trading

Options provide a good testing ground where you can learn swing trading, making real trades. One reason they are good to use is the cost of investing is small, the potential losses are self-limited, and potential profits are high.

You can begin by investing from $100-$300.

When investing, you can try out different time horizons. This can get you used to tracking the markets over time periods of days, weeks, and a month or so. This will help you develop as a swing trader and come upon a strategy that you can use over the long term.

Buying Puts and Calls

Another advantage of using options to get started is you can learn how to short or bet against the market. That is profit from downturns. Put contracts provide a very easy way to do this. You can also learn about hedging since you can use puts to mitigate the risk of investing in call options.

Looking at a specific example, consider the stock AMD. The current share price is $26.60. A $27 call expiring on May 31 costs $1. Since it represents 100 shares, if we buy one contract, it would cost $100. To buy some insurance against a possible loss, we can buy a cheap put contract on AMD that expires on the same date. A $25 put is available for $0.77, so it would cost $77. Even cheaper puts are available, for example, we could get a $23.50 put for $37 total.

To review, the way this would work, if the price of AMD goes above $27, then we would profit off the call. The put option would expire worthlessly.

Let's say that at 7 days to expiration, AMD rises to $30 a share. The call option would be worth $3. That is per share, so we could sell the call option on the market for $300. The put option would be completely worthless under those circumstances. Our profit would be $123. Not bad, making a $123 profit on a $177 investment. If we had simply bought the call option by itself, we would have made a 123% profit. Suppose the share price instead dipped to $23. The $25 put would be worth $2, so we could sell it on the market for $200. Our original investment was $177 – so we made a small profit.

Chapter 8: FOREX Trading Basics

FOREX is a very popular way to get into day and swing trading. Forex stands for foreign exchange. It's where the world's currencies are traded against one another. The daily volume traded on the currency exchange is far larger than that traded in the stock markets, by orders of magnitude. Currency trading is becoming increasingly popular among "retail" traders, which are amateurs like you just getting into trading. Many people are making large sums off it.

In short, Forex trading involves buying one currency and selling another in order to make profits. Supply and demand drive prices on the Forex markets just like they do anything else. With time, different currencies are in more demand than others and so their prices go up. Prices go down when traders are selling off a currency.

How Currency is Traded

Currency is traded in lots of 1,000 units. This is called a micro-lot. If you are trading in dollars, a micro-lot will be $1,000. A mini-lot will be $10,000, and a standard lot size is $100,000.

Currencies are traded in pairs. This makes currency trading a little different than stock trading. On the stock market, you can buy Amazon (say) and then you can sell Amazon.

On the Forex market, you can only trade in pairs so you could buy Euros with dollars and then buy Japanese Yen with Euros, but you can't just buy Euros and then sell Euros. Prices on Forex are quoted in terms of the price of one currency against another. So, you could see the price of the dollar against the British pound or the price of the dollar against the Euro. Again, this is different from the stock market where prices are given in terms of individual stocks, rather than pricing stocks against one another.

You also need to know how currency prices are listed. They are priced to the fourth decimal place. A pip is defined to be one one-hundredth of 100%. The acronym means the point in percentage.

Prices of currency pairs are listed as the pair symbols with the price it would take to use the second currency to buy the first currency. For example, EUR/JPY would give the price in Japanese Yen to buy one Euro, which is currently 123.29 Japanese Yen. As another example, EUR/USD would be the price in dollars to buy one Euro, which is 1.1239. Note that while most currencies are tracked to the fourth decimal place, the Japanese Yen is only tracked to two decimal places.

In order to determine the inverse, that is how many Euros it would take to buy one Japanese Yen or how many Euros it would take to buy one US dollar; you divide 1 by the quoted value. So, it would take $1/123.29 = 0.0081$ Euros to buy one Japanese Yen. Doing the same for the dollar, it would take 1/1.1239 = 0.8898 Euros to buy one dollar.

During the week, currency trading goes on all over the world. So, it's taking place 24 hours a day in different markets, including Europe, Asia, and the Americas. As a result, prices are constantly fluctuating.

Profits in Pips

Currency moves are tracked in pips. So, if the currency pair EUR/USD was at 1.1840 and it changed to 1.1880, we'd say there was a 40 pip move. If you had bought it when it was 1.1840 and sold at 1.1880, we'd also say that you earned a 40-pip profit. However, the actual profits are in terms of lots. For a micro-lot, a one pip move translates into $0.10. In the example given, a 40-pip move would result in a profit of $4 per micro-lot. If we had a mini lot instead, one pip would translate into a $1 move. So, the profit of 40 pips would translate into a profit of $40 per mini-lot. Finally, for a standard lot, one pip corresponds to $10. So, a profit of 40 pips would be $400 per standard lot.

Naturally, there can be corresponding losses, in the same absolute amounts. So, if the trade went the other way, that is supposing that we bought the currency pair at 1.1880 but had to sell it at 1.1840, that would be a 40 pip loss, and a standard loss would have lost $400.

When computing pips involving trades with Japanese Yen, multiplication by 100 is required.

Currency Pairs and Charts

The leading currency in a currency pair is used as the directional currency in a chart. That is, if you are trading EUR/USD, in the chart describing the currency pair, the Euro will move with the trend. Upward trends in the chart would correspond to rising prices of the Euro relative to the dollar, and vice versa.

Swing Trading Forex

Forex markets have high volatility. So, swing trading on Forex will require the use of stop-losses to ensure you don't get wiped out. When swing trading on Forex, you will hold your trades for several days or more.

Chapter 9: Top Beginner Mistakes

Swing trading, like any other type of trading, carries some risk with it. Anyone can mess up a trade, but beginners are more prone to mistakes. In this short guide, we will attempt to lay out some common mistakes made by beginning traders and how you might avoid them.

Having unrealistic expectations

You may be getting into swing trading thinking that you can make a full-time income. The truth is that you can. However, it's not something that is going to happen automatically. It takes time to learn the tricks of the trade and to learn how to properly trade in order to make profits on a consistent basis. You should also not have unrealistic expectations about the amount of money you will earn in the beginning. You probably aren't going to make a million dollars on your first trade.

Not treating trading like a business

Some people view the stock market as a gambling casino. But it's not a gambling casino at all, and the techniques described in this book are not designed to "beat" the system. They are rooting in the mathematics that underlies the operation of markets. In any case, when you become a swing trader and intend to earn a full-time living from it, this is a business. You need to treat it the way that you would treat any other business. Many new traders think of it in terms of making a fast buck without balancing the books and taking it as seriously as it needs to be taken. If they opened a McDonald's, they'd be far more careful. You should treat it exactly the way you would if you opened a restaurant or a consulting firm. Most people would approach such ventures with far more care, and if you can do so with your trading business, while you might not make a million dollars the first month, you will be on a sustained path to deriving real income.

Being too anxious

Being a successful swing trader requires patience. You will hold onto your investments for several days to possibly weeks, and some swing traders even hold onto their trades for months. This can be difficult for people that are impatient. Another way that being too anxious can get in the way is that anxious traders simply go out and make trades that feel good but have no analysis behind them. That might work out now and then when you get lucky, but over time, that is a recipe for failure.

Failing to Plan

This brings us to our second beginner mistake – failing to plan. We've described a large number of useful tools in this book, and we're only scratching the surface although we've discussed the most popular ones. Before going into a trade, you should study the security you hope to trade and make a plan to carry out the trade. Your plan should include your entry point, how much profit you will take, how much loss you're going to accept, and your exit plan. You shouldn't go in on a hunch and should instead study various securities to see which ones will work out to serve your interests the best.

Looking for a get rich quick scheme

Many people go into trading thinking that they can get rich quick. This simply isn't true. Yes, sometimes it happens. But most of the time, it doesn't. People are surprised to find out that trading takes work and time invested in study. It is not the get rich quick scheme or gambling casino that people imagine. If you are looking for a get rich quick scheme, you are setting yourself up for losses, because your mentality will lead you to try and cut corners in search of profits. When you do that, mistakes are likely to be made.

Being put off by all that math

There is a fair amount of math involved behind the scenes, and wall street is full of people with math and physics degrees that are working behind the scenes on formulas, coming up with new derivatives contracts, or coming up with new tricks like special moving averages. However, as a trader, you don't need to get involved at that level of detail. While you will have to get some comfort level with math, it is not necessary to go all in. Take your time and study slowly. Nobody is going to start the first day and understand all the charts and moving averages. However, to successfully trade options, the trader must be able to use and understand the charts. You don't have to understand how moving averages are calculated, but you need to understand how to look at the charts and understanding what they mean on a practical level.

Losing control with leverage

Swing traders on the stock market have access to leverage. That is, you can borrow from the brokerage at a 2:1 ratio. This can get some people into trouble. There is no faster path to debt than playing with other people's money. Leverage can also lead some people to take risks that they wouldn't otherwise take. At the beginning of your swing trading career, you should consider trading without using leverage. Save that until later when you're more experienced and less likely to make huge, costly mistakes.

Not relying on multiple indicators

Earlier, we had detailed discussions of tools and indicators that can be used to determine when to buy and sell. One common mistake made by beginners is to see a buy or sell signal in one indicator and get anxious and either enter or exit their position. Sometimes that will work, but to protect yourself, you need to use more than one indicator before making any moves. The cold reality is that no one indicator is right all the time. When you see a buy or sell signal, confirm it before making your trade.

Chapter 10: How Much Money Do You Need to Get Started

An important issue that many beginners want to know is how much money they need to get started. In this chapter, we will have a look at reasonable capital requirements and also discuss the use of leverage, which will let you borrow from the brokerage.

Minimal Capital Requirements

The old saying goes you need to have money to make money. But is that really true? Well, it is to some degree, but maybe not as much as you're expecting. You probably aren't going to be able to do many swing trades digging quarters out of your couch. That said, the amount of capital required to start dipping your toes in the water doesn't amount to a huge amount of money.

The first thing to note, which we've touched on a bit already, is that swing trading isn't bound by the same constraints as day trading. A day trade is a specific position that is opened and closed on the same trading day. To become a day trader, you have to get approved by your broker. People that day trade have day trading accounts, and day traders are locked in with specific capital requirements. The minimal requirement most brokerages have is $25,000 cash.

Brokerages do this because day trading is considered a very high-risk activity. That isn't to say everyone who day trades loses their shirt, but those that succeed in day trading are very careful and methodical traders who spend a great deal of time studying the market.

Remember that brokerages will designate you as a day trader if you make 4 or more-day trades within any 5-day trading period. You could get by making 3-day trades in a 5-day period without the day trader designation, but if you are pursuing swing trading, then it should not be necessary to make those kinds of trades. The only situation where you should close a position on the same trading day if you're a swing trader is in the special case that the stock makes a sudden profitable move that would allow you to book huge profits. In our view, you shouldn't "wing it" in these situations, you should set up sell limit orders that automate this process for you. Set a rule on how much of a change to the upside you want to trigger a sale and place the order. Generally, large moves like that are rare so its not going to happen very often, and if you are following the techniques of swing trading, you've probably entered your position days before some event (like an unexpectedly upbeat earnings report) has triggered a sell condition.

Of course, you need to be just as serious with swing trading – but swing trading is a lower risk activity. That isn't to say you can't blow a large amount of money swing trading, you absolutely can. But because it's a more careful type of trading, you aren't trying to unload everything in the heat of the moment in the middle of the day — it's considered to be a more moderate risk activity.

So, let's get to the bottom line. Since swing trading isn't regulated in the same way, the amount of capital you need to get started is going to depend on your goals and trading style. We advise that you start small. In fact, many stock trading sites have simulated systems you can practice on. You can enter into trades that aren't real (i.e., don't use real money and aren't actually executed by a broker) but they work in real time as if they were real. So, you can do a simulated trade and see how it works out. Spending a month or so doing this type of simulation will help you train before going out and doing actual trades. Many people will be too impatient to do this, but you wouldn't go out and play for a football team without training first – so why wouldn't you do the same here?

After your month of simulation training, we recommend starting out with small amounts of capital if you've never done real-time trades. This advice will be ignored by the impatient, but everyone should be cautious when starting out. Begin by trading older companies that have more stable share prices over the time frames used for swing trading. You should also start out with less than $1,000 and only trade a few shares at a time, to get used to the process.

Consider Options Trading

Not everyone wants to trade options, but we recommend putting some capital toward trading options at least in the beginning. The main reason is that you can begin trading options with hardly any capital. People are put off by options because there is a lot of sophisticated lingoes associated with them, but once you take some time to read up and study options, you'll discover that they really aren't all that complicated. The only capital that is put at risk is the premium, and often you can trade options for under $100. Trading options can be lucrative in itself, but if that is not your long-term goal, you should still consider doing it for a month. That way, you can get used to reading stock market data and charts and using tools like moving averages to make your picks. It's a little bit more complicated than stocks because of the expiration dates, but that also enforces a swing trading mentality. An option is not going to be something you're going to hold for very long; you are looking to book your profits in a matter of days or weeks. Options trading can be done at low cost and even commission-free on some platforms like tastytrade or Robinhood. Find the platform you like best and use that. Tastytrade is good for educational purposes.

Planning for Risk

Ultimately, the amount of capital you need will depend on two factors. The first is the amount of capital that you can comfortably put up to invest. As mentioned before, if you won't be able to pay your mortgage because you're pouring money into the markets, then you're putting too much money up. The rule of thumb to apply is that you should put up an amount of money that you can afford to lose completely. That doesn't mean it wouldn't be painful to lose the money, but you should be able to pay your basic living expenses in the event that you lost all of it. But frankly, you would have to be an impulsive and careless trader to lose every dime with swing trading that just shouldn't happen.

The second factor is your tolerance level for risk. The standard recommendation, as noted earlier, is 1% per trade. Many others recommend 2%. It is possible to risk more in the beginning, provided you have an outside source where you can replenish the capital. We suggest this because, in the beginning, you might only have $500 to invest, period, but we believe that shouldn't constrain you from getting in the same and learning the trade.

With a 2% risk level, that means if you have $10,000 in your account, then you can risk $200.

Whatever risk level you decide to go with, make that a rule for each trade. To enforce the rule, you will use a stop-loss order with each trade. Simply saying you're only going to risk 2% isn't going to work, because when you're in the heat of the actual trades, emotions can take over. What often happens is that when an investment is going bad, people start getting consumed with hope and fear simultaneously, and then their judgment starts to go south. In practice, this means that you'll hold onto a losing investment a lot longer than you should and lose a lot more capital.

The first step is to determine the number of shares you will trade. You can work backward or forward on this one. Let's say that you're going to trade a stock that is currently $50 a share. If you decide that you want to place your stop-loss order at $49, the trade risk is $1. Trade risk is given by the amount per share that you are willing to risk. If your account is $10,000 and your risk tolerance is 2%, then your total amount to lose is $200, and so you can buy:

Total risk per trade/trade risk per share = $200/$1 = 200 shares

Well golly, that would be your entire $10,000! Of course, in most cases, you're not going to put your entire principal on one trade, but with the stop-loss order in place, it would be pretty low risk. In a worst-case scenario, you'd end up with $9,800. However, it's important to note that in many situations, it will be reasonable to put all your money on a single trade. We can think of several examples. Suppose that Samsung or Apple is about to release a slick new phone or issue an earnings report that people are expecting is going to be stellar. There is always some risk, investors are often disappointed by new product releases, and the earnings report might actually fail to meet or beat expectations. However, such events are often followed by big stock rallies.

Another case where a large investment might be warranted is when you're investing in an index fund. Key times to make these types of investments often fit around the release of jobs reports or release of GDP numbers. When these data released by the government turn out to be good numbers, large stock market rallies follow. Of course, your timing in these kinds of trades will be critical. It's possible to get in the day before and book large profits, however.

At other times, the market will be rising because of other reasons; maybe the economy is just in a growth spurt. These are also good times to load up on one index fund. In order to determine when there is a good time to enter the trade, you will use the tools discussed in this book. So, you will spend time looking at moving averages, candles, and Bollinger bands. When you see a strong buy, signal confirmed by multiple indicators, then you can enter your trade.

Bottom Line – How Much Do You Need?

Since there are no specific requirements to become a swing trader, the amount you need is a personal decision. You can do a quick analysis as we did above to see what you could risk with an account that has $X. You will also want to look at the stocks that you're interested in trading. Amazon is trading over $1,800 per share at the time of writing. AMD, on the other hand, is trading at $27 a share. Amazon is a stronger company, but obviously, you're going to be looking at different stop-loss levels for stocks that are priced so differently.

When making your trades, most of the time you'll want to leave money in the account so that you can pursue multiple trades, with the possible exceptions of the scenarios we painted above.

So, there is no hard answer to this question. It's something that you'll need to determine for your own personal situation. You can start with trading as little as one share, but we'd recommend going with a service like Robinhood if you decide to do that because you won't want your tiny trades to be eaten alive by commissions. You might wait until you can put at least $500 before getting started, but you can use trades as small as you like to get used to the process and methods.

Using Leverage

Swing traders can access leverage from their brokers. The first concept to understand is margin. While it sounds mysterious, margin is simply borrowing funds from the broker so that you can make larger trades. Not everyone is going to be able to do this, and your financial fitness will be evaluated before the broker will allow you to borrow to make trades.

Leverage is generated by margin. What leverage means is simply that you can trade a larger amount than you could using your own principal. Leverage is described in terms of ratios. So if leverage is given as 3:1, that would mean that if you had $10,000 in your account, you would be able to borrow from the broker such that you could make a $30,000 trade or enter multiple trades that summed up to $30,000. Obviously, this approach carries some risk and a very large risk, indeed. If the trades you enter completely go south, you could end up not only losing your principal but also owing the broker a large amount of money.

Swing traders by convention can use 2:1 leverage. So, if you have $15,000 in your account, you would be able to buy $30,000 worth of stock. Forex traders can use 50:1 leverage.

Leverage is risky, but it also can multiply profits. Suppose that a stock is trading at $20 a share and they are about to release a new smartphone everyone believes will take the market by storm. Without leverage, if you have a $10,000 account, you can buy $10,000/$20 = 500 shares. Suppose they release the phone and it has a surprise feature everyone wants so the stock doubles in price over some time period. You close your position at $40 a share. Your total revenue is $20,000. Less your original investment of $10,000, you made a $10,000 profit. You doubled your money – an unusual situation for sure, but it could happen. And it's happening now for the sake of example.

Suppose that you used leverage and at 2:1, were able to buy $20,000 worth of stock, borrowing $10,000 from the broker. That means you would have been able to purchase 1,000 shares rather than just 500. After all is said and done, you'd have 1,000 shares x $40/share = $40,000. You pay back the broker the $10,000 you borrowed, leaving you with $30,000. You've earned a $20,000 profit since you started out with $10,000 in the account. By using 2:1 margin, you doubled your profits (surprise!).

You can also magnify your losses. What if instead, the company announced that it was canceling the phone and the share price dropped from $20 to $9 a share. If you had invested your own money, you'd end up with $9 x 500 = $4,500 so end up losing $5,500.

Had you borrowed the $10,000 from the broker, you'd have $9 x 1,000 shares = $9,000 left over. And you owe the broker $10,000. So, your account would be wiped out. You'd have to deposit money from external sources to settle with the broker and hopefully restore some principal to the account.

Of course, this example illustrates the value of stop-loss orders. If you had put a stop-loss order of $19, then you would have ended up with $19 x 1,000 shares = $19,000. You'd be able to pay the broker back the $10,000 and have $9,000 left in your trading account. A loss, but not a catastrophic loss.

One Danger with Stop-Loss Orders

Many advisors suggest putting stop-loss orders on the order of 10 cents or 50 cents. Honestly, this is too conservative. If you've noticed something from all the discussions about data in this book, you realize that financial instruments don't always move smoothly in one direction. They zigzag in jagged fashion on their way to the top (if they are going up). If your stop loss order is too conservative, you might get thrown out of a position too early when there is a retracement. You probably don't want that to happen – but the level you put for your stop-loss order is a personal decision based on your own financial situation and risk tolerance. However, always use stop-loss orders. That is a critical lesson. Better to protect yourself from some level of loss than lose it all.

Chapter 11: Exchange-Traded Funds

We've decided to put in a special chapter on exchange-traded funds because these offer a special opportunity for beginner investors. Exchange-traded funds are often described as mutual funds that trade like stocks. That is true as far as it goes, but exchange-traded funds also allow you to do a lot more than you can just buy individual stocks. You can track indexes, like the Dow Jones Industrial Average, S & P 500, or Russell 3000. You can also invest in overseas markets using exchange-traded funds. Another huge benefit is they allow you to utilize the stock market to invest in commodities, real estate, and other assets that you wouldn't normally be able to trade as stock. Using gold as an example, an exchange-traded fund works in the following way. A brokerage buys up a bunch of gold. Then they issue shares for ownership. Then as the price of gold fluctuates, you can profit from that without having actually to own the gold. Of course, with such an arrangement, you can't take physical ownership of the gold, your only rights are to the shares so you can buy shares or sell shares and profit. But as a trader, you are probably not interested in actually owning the gold anyway. So, exchange-traded funds are an exciting way to get swing trading on the stock market while at the same time in a virtual sense trading on many different markets. Exchange-traded funds are often known as ETFs.

Where to Buy Exchange-Traded Funds

Buying exchange-traded funds is simply a matter of knowing the ticker symbol and trading them on the stock market. There are many funds available offered by different companies, but two of the most popular are iShares and State Street SPDR. Before investing in a particular fund, you'll want to look it up and examine different factors such as historical returns. Although different companies will offer the same product on the surface, they won't perform the same way because the investments may be weighted. For example, I could make up a fund made up of Amazon, Google, and Facebook and call it the AGF exchange-traded fund. Then I could buy 1,000 shares of each and then divide up the total into shares of my own that investors could buy. In this scenario, each company's share price would have an equal impact on the share price of my AGF fund. Someone else could offer a fund based on the same underlying companies, but they could weight them differently. Let's call their fund AMOG. Suppose that in their fund, they buy 2,000 shares of Amazon, 1,000 shares of Google, and 500 shares of Facebook. Due to the different weights, their fund will have different historical performance as time goes on.

So, you'll need to look at individual funds in each case that you're interested in. For example, SPDR, iShares, and Vanguard all offer ETFs that track the S&P 500, but they may not perform in exactly the same way or have the same share prices.

Trading Options on Exchange-Traded Funds

Remember that in every sense of the word, an exchange-traded fund is a stock. That means you can trade options. This opens up some interesting scenarios. For example, SPDR offers an exchange-traded fund for gold, with ticker GLD. You can trade options on this fund, so you're basically trading options on gold. Technically that isn't true, but it's the basic reality. You're trading options on the changing price of gold and investor sentiment on gold. You can do this for anything that an ETF is based on, including real estate or consumer staples and natural resources. Currency ETFs are also available so you can trade ETFs based on FOREX as well.

iShares and SPDR

As we've noted, you should compare funds offered by different companies to find the ones that fit in with your plan as far as to share price and historical performance. However, for the sake of demonstrating what is available in

ETF investing, we will look at iShares specifically. You can visit the company at iShares.com. State Street can be found at spdrs.com.

ETFs are offered in the following distinct asset classes:

- Equity (stocks)
- Fixed income (bonds)
- Commodity
- Real estate

Global funds are available for the United States. First, let us have a look at some of the offerings in a commodity. There are 358 different funds offered by iShares with six funds for commodities, including for gold and silver. The GSG fund gives you a broad exposure to commodities that even includes the livestock and energy sectors.

You can also buy shares in ETFs that track major indices of the stock market. Common choices offered by SPDR include DIA, which tracks the Dow Jones Industrial Average, SPY, which tracks the S & P 500, and SPSM tracks small caps. You can also invest in many different sectors. For example, XLV can be used to invest in healthcare while XLE invests in the energy sector.

ETFs are also available that are set up according to asset allocation. With bonds, you can invest in everything from junk bonds ('high yield') to US Treasuries.

Summary

Investing in ETFs may be something you are interested in or not, but they offer several advantages. The first is automatic diversification. You can find funds to invest in different sectors, different company sizes, and different markets. You can also invest in hard assets like gold without actually having to buy and sell actual gold, and you can invest in bonds as if they were stocks. Another advantage is being able to track market indexes. You could go out and buy shares in all 500 companies making up the S&P 500, but that would take an enormous amount of capital. SPY saves you the trouble. Tracking indices isn't as exciting as trading FOREX or individual stocks, but over time can generate as much or more profits.

Another advantage of ETFs is they give you access to foreign markets without the associated risks of investing directly. Investing in foreign markets can carry a great deal of risk, as some foreign markets lack the legal protections that US markets offer investors, and some are unregulated. In addition, currency exchange may be necessary to invest in overseas markets, making it more difficult to carry out investments and leaving you with losses that might be incurred by currency shifts. Using ETFs removes all of those risks allowing you to invest in Europe, Japan, Latin

America, or Asia as if they were nothing more than regular stocks traded in the United States.

Conclusion

Thank you for taking the time to read *Swing Trading 2019: Beginners Guide to Best Strategies, Tools, Tactics and Psychology to Profit from Outstanding Short-Term Trading Opportunities on Stock Market, Options, Forex, and Cryptocurrencies.* We hope that you've found the book informative and educational and that the information presented herein will help you develop your own trading plans and become a successful swing trader. We sincerely wish all readers the best of luck in their trades! If you found this book useful, please drop by Amazon and leave an informative and constructive review. We really appreciate the help!

Swing trading is a strategy that attempts to take advantage of price swings in the markets. The goal is to buy low and sell high, realizing profits from trades that last 2 days up to several months in time frames. There are no hard rules about the time frames you use, that is up to each investor. However, to be swing trading, you will have to hold your trades at least overnight. Many people attracted to active investing are not patient enough to do this, but rewards are available for those who can master this strategy. Swing trading has a goal of realizing capital now, while long-term investors seek to build up their investments over decades. To be successful at swing trading, you will have to beat the market in performance. If you don't do so, then you might as well park your money in a mutual fund and wait for the returns. The good news is that many swing traders do beat the markets and earn a very substantial income from swing trading. It's entirely possible to earn a six or seven figure income from swing trading but remember that most people will fail to do so and no results are typical. But if you are dedicated and work on it daily and keep your discipline, it's entirely possible to enter the ranks of the successful.

Swing trading offers a great opportunity for small investors to become traders and rapidly grow their own trading business. Unlike day trading, the risk is somewhat mitigated since you're not making trades by the hour or even by the minute. The stress level is a lot lower, and you don't have to be hunched over your computer all day every day in case you need to do a quick sell off or place a buy order. For those who are interested in taking an active role in their investing but either don't have the time to work on it full-time right now or the inclination to do so, swing trading offers a solid middle ground between conservative, long-term investing and day trading. Moreover, swing trading doesn't have any capital requirements. You can get started as large or small as you like, rather than having to deposit $25,000 as you would be required to do for day trading. Swing trading also offers a training ground if you actually do want to become a day trader. It can offer you the experience you need to be a successful day trader without the time pressure so you can learn how to correctly utilize indicators and other tools that you would use while day trading. And this can be done under far less pressure. You can also use swing trading as a springboard into day trading. In other words, if you want to be a day trader, but can't deposit the amount required and don't have much trading experience and so draw a skeptical eye from your broker, you can use swing trading to raise the capital and to gain valuable trading experience.

Perhaps the biggest advantage of swing trading is that the techniques are entirely general. So you can use swing trading techniques on the stock market, with Forex trading, trading futures or commodities, with cryptocurrency, or trading options. You can stick to one of these that you are interested in or trade in all of them. Whichever path you take, we wish you the best of luck and hope you earn high profits!

CPSIA information can be obtained
at www.ICGtesting.com
Printed in the USA
LVHW080829141020
668357LV00047B/259

9 781953 693464